Java™ 2, v5.0 (Tiger) New Features

About the Author

Herbert Schildt is a leading authority on the Java, C, C++, and C# languages, and is a master Windows programmer. His programming books have sold more than 3 million copies worldwide and have been translated into all major foreign languages. He is the author of the best selling *Java 2: The Complete Reference* and *Java 2: A Beginner's Guide.* Among his other bestsellers are *C++: The Complete Reference, C++: A Beginner's Guide, C#: The Complete Reference,* and *C#: A Beginner's Guide.* Schildt holds a master's degree in computer science from the University of Illinois. He can be reached at his consulting office at (217) 586-4683. His Web site is **www.HerbSchildt.com**.

Java™ 2, v5.0 (Tiger) New Features

Herbert Schildt

McGraw-Hill/Osborne

New York   Chicago   San Francisco
Lisbon   London   Madrid   Mexico City   Milan
New Delhi   San Juan   Seoul   Singapore   Sydney   Toronto

The McGraw-Hill Companies

McGraw-Hill/Osborne
2100 Powell Street, 10th Floor
Emeryville, California 94608
U.S.A.

To arrange bulk purchase discounts for sales promotions, premiums, or fund-raisers, please contact **McGraw-Hill**/Osborne at the above address. For information on translations or book distributors outside the U.S.A., please see the International Contact Information page immediately following the index of this book.

Java™ 2, v5.0 (Tiger) New Features

1234567890 CUS CUS 01987654

ISBN 0-07-225854-3

Publisher	Brandon A. Nordin
Vice President & Associate Publisher	Scott Rogers
Acquisitions Editor	Lisa McClain
Project Editor	Janet Walden
Acquisitions Coordinator	Athena Honore
Technical Editor	James Holmes
Copy Editor	William McManus
Proofreader	Claire Splan
Indexer	Sheryl Schildt
Composition	Jim Kussow, Jean Butterfield
Series Designer	Peter F. Hancik
Cover Designer	Pattie Lee

This book was composed with Corel VENTURA™ Publisher.

Contents at a Glance

Contents

Introduction

Since its inception, Java has been at the core of a culture of change and innovation. Beginning with its original 1.0 release, it radically altered the way that we program for the Internet. Building on the well-known syntax of C/C++, Java streamlined the object model, simplified memory management, and added built-in support for multithreading. Today, we take these features for granted, but nearly a decade ago, they were fundamental and far-reaching advances.

Of course, version 1.0 was just the beginning for Java. Over the intervening years, Java has continued to grow, evolve, and otherwise redefine itself. Unlike many other languages, which are slow to incorporate new features, Java has continually been at the forefront of computer language design. One reason for this is its culture of innovation and change. As a result, Java has gone through several upgrades—some relatively small, but others quite large.

Of these revisions, Java 2, v5.0 ranks as the most significant change to Java since its original release. So profound are its additions that they will forever alter the way that Java code is written. For example, generics fundamentally expand and alter Java's syntax, autoboxing simplifies the interplay between primitive types and objects, and metadata adds an entirely new programming dimension. Given the nature of the innovation, it is no surprise that the code name for the Java 2 Platform, Standard Edition, Version 5.0 (J2SE 5.0) was "Tiger" during its development.

This book describes the many new features that have been incorporated into the Java language with the advent of Java 2, v5.0. It is intended for experienced Java programmers who want to get up to speed as quickly as possible on "the new Java." Because it describes only the features added by Java 2, v5.0, you won't have to wade through reams of material you already know. Thus, this book is about only one thing: what's new in Java!

What Software Was Used

The code and information in this book was verified and tested against Java 2, Standard Edition, Version 5.0 (J2SE 5.0), Beta 2, which reflects a stable feature-set.

How to Get Java 2, v5.0

Java 2, v5.0 is available free of charge from Sun's Web site, **www.java.sun.com**. Simply download J2SE 5.0.

Don't Forget: Code on the Web

Remember, the source code for all of the examples in this book is available free of charge on the Web at **www.osborne.com**.

More from Herb Schildt

Java 2, v5.0 (Tiger) New Features is just one in the Herb Schildt series of programming books. Here are some other titles that you will find of interest.

To learn more about Java, we recommend the following:

Java 2: The Complete Reference

The Art of Java (co-authored with James Holmes)

Java 2: A Beginner's Guide

To learn about C++ programming, you will find these books especially helpful:

C++: The Complete Reference

C++: A Beginner's Guide

Teach Yourself C++

C++ from the Ground Up

STL Programming from the Ground Up

To learn about C#, we suggest the following books:

C#: A Beginner's Guide

C#: The Complete Reference

If you want to learn about the C language, the foundation of all modern programming, then the following titles will be of interest:

C: The Complete Reference

Teach Yourself C

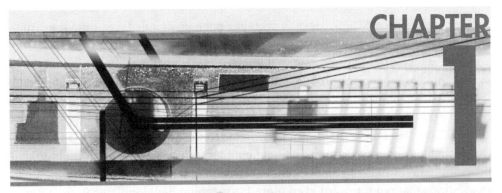

CHAPTER

1

The Tiger Is Loose

Codenamed "Tiger," Java 2, v5.0 has once again put Java at the forefront of computer language design. Unlike most of the previous Java upgrades, which offered important, but incremental improvements, version 5.0 *fundamentally expands the scope, power, and range* of the language. Not since its original launch nearly a decade ago has a release of Java been so important, or so eagerly awaited.

Java 2, v5.0 contains major enhancements to the Java language. Many of these, such as generics, autoboxing, and enumerations, have been desired by Java programmers for many years. Others, such as metadata, are forward-thinking innovations that point toward even more far-reaching developments in the future. In both cases, they will fundamentally affect the way that all Java programmers write code.

This book describes the new features of Java 2, v5.0. It is expressly for programmers who already know Java and who want to get up to speed as quickly as possible with its many innovations. It does not teach the basics of Java, nor does it rehash older material. Instead, this book focuses exclusively on the changes to Java brought about by Java 2, v5.0. In short, if you are an experienced Java programmer wanting to move as quickly as possible to Java 2, v5.0, this book is for you.

Overview of Changes

Before beginning an in-depth examination of the new features in Java 2, v5.0, an overview will be of value. Not only will this give you a sense of the scope of the additions, but it will also give you a general understanding of how the new features relate to one another and, in many cases, work together.

Here is a list of the major new features:

- Generics
- Metadata
- Autoboxing/unboxing
- Enumerations

- Enhanced, for-each style **for** loop
- Variable-length arguments (varargs)
- Static import
- Formatted I/O
- Upgrades to the API

As you can see, this is not a list of minor tweaks or incremental upgrades. Each item in the list represents a significant addition to the Java language. Some, such as generics, the enhanced **for**, and varargs, introduce new syntax elements. Others, such as autoboxing and auto-unboxing, alter the semantics of the language. Metadata adds an entirely new dimension to programming. In all cases, substantial functionality has been added.

The following sections present an overview of each major new feature.

Generics

Generics have been long awaited by Java programmers. At its core, the term *generics* means *parameterized types*. Parameterized types are important because they enable the programmer to create generic methods, classes, and interfaces, in which the type of data upon which they operate is specified as a parameter. With generics, it is possible to create a single class, for example, that automatically works with different types of data. Thus, generics expand the programmer's ability to re-use code. As a point of reference, generics in Java are somewhat similar to templates in C++.

In addition to promoting code reuse, generics add type safety. Because the generics mechanism implicitly handles type conversions, explicit casts are not required. Furthermore, type mismatches are caught at compile time, rather than at run time. This means that run-time casting errors are avoided.

Generics represent a major change to the core of the Java language. Their addition required an entirely new syntax element, for example. The expressive power they add to the language is profoundly changing the way that Java code is written.

Metadata

The new metadata facility lets you embed annotations into a program. The annotations are then processed by various programming tools. For example, a tool might generate Java source code as requested by an annotation. The Java metadata facility is part of a growing trend in programming in which the programmer specifies an action but leaves it to a tool to actually provide the code. Such an approach reduces the amount of repetitious code that a programmer must enter by hand.

Autoboxing and Auto-Unboxing

Autoboxing is the feature that lets Java automatically encapsulate a primitive type, such as an **int**, in a class. Auto-unboxing is the reverse process; a primitive type represented by a class is automatically converted into its corresponding primitive type. Because they streamline many common programming operations, autoboxing and auto-unboxing are additions that all Java programmers will welcome.

Enumerations

In essence, an *enumeration* is a list of named constants. The enumeration type is supported by the new keyword **enum**. In the past, when such constants were needed, they were typically coded as **static final**. An enumeration offers a much better alternative. In Java, **enum** declares a class type, which means that an **enum** can have methods and fields. This gives **enum** capabilities in Java that surpass its counterpart in other languages (such as C++).

Enhanced for Loop

Java 2, v5.0 adds a "for-each" capability to the **for** loop. This enhancement lets the **for** cycle through the contents of a collection or an array, from beginning to end, with ease. In programming, such tasks are quite common. This new for-each feature not only simplifies such loops, but makes them safer, too, by preventing boundary errors.

Varargs

Varargs, which is short for *variable-length arguments,* is a new feature that lets a method take a variable number of arguments. The addition of varargs makes it easier to create methods whose argument list varies from call to call.

Formatted I/O

Java 2, v5.0 offers an alternative way to input or output formatted data through the use of the new **Formatter** and **Scanner** classes. **Formatter** formats information for output. **Scanner** reads formatted input. For output, you can also use the new **printf( )** method, which is based on the well-known C language **printf( )** function.

Static Import

The static import feature streamlines access to the static members within a class. When using static import, it is possible to refer to static members directly by their names, without having to qualify them with their class names. For example, prior to the static import facility, a method in Java's math library needed to be qualified with the **Math** class, as in **Math.cos( )**. With static import, the program can import the static members of **Math** and then refer to the static methods directly, as in **cos( )**.

Changes to the Collections Framework and Other Parts of the API

The Java Collections Framework provides off-the-shelf solutions to a wide variety of common programming problems that pertain to groups of objects. For example, the Collections Framework supplies classes that implement lists, sets, and maps. Java 2, v5.0 completely updates this powerful subsystem so that it takes advantage of generics and autoboxing. This makes using collections both easier and safer. Java 2, v5.0 also updates the Collections classes for use by the enhanced **for** loop. Accompanying these major changes are many smaller, but valuable enhancements that further expand the power and applicability of the Collections Framework.

Other parts of the API have also been affected by the move to generics. For example, **Class**, one of the original Java 1.0 classes, is now generic. The retrofitting of generics into selected classes and methods enhances the power of the libraries by offering type safety and enabling better type checking.

In addition to upgrading to generics, Java 2, v5.0 adds other important new functionality to the library. The two most important are support for metadata (annotations) and a new concurrent programming API.

A Culture of Innovation

As the preceding discussion suggests, the additions to Java are quite significant. Instead of simply tweaking a feature here or adjusting a nuance there, Java 2, v5.0 fundamentally expands the language. This level of innovation is seldom seen in a language as mature and widely used as Java. In general, computer languages usually follow a "life cycle" that begins with a burst of creativity and innovation, followed by a long period of widespread use and stability, and ending with the language being used to maintain "legacy" code. Java is now in the middle period of its life cycle. It would normally be settling down into a long period of tranquility, resting on its laurels, so to speak. But Java isn't following the rules!

Since the beginning, Java has been at the center of a culture of innovation. Its original release redefined programming for the Internet world. The Java Virtual Machine (JVM) and bytecode changed the way we think about security and portability. The applet (and then the servlet) made the Web come alive. The Java Community Process (JCP) redefined the way that new ideas are assimilated into the language. It should come as no surprise that Java continues to push the frontiers of programming.

With the release of Java 2, v5.0, the world of Java programming has changed. Many of the techniques that you have relied on in the past have become outdated, being replaced by better, more powerful constructs. Programmers who fail to adopt the new strategies will soon find themselves left behind. Frankly, in the competitive world of programming, no Java programmer can afford to be left behind. The purpose of this book is to speed your transition to the new Java.

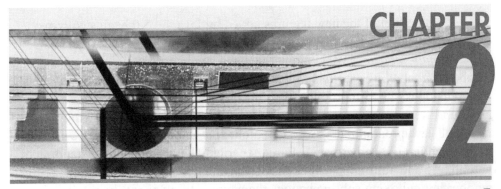

CHAPTER

2

Autoboxing and
Auto-Unboxing

Exploration of the new features added by Java 2, v5.0 begins with two that have been long awaited by Java programmers: *autoboxing* and *auto-unboxing.* We begin with these features for three reasons. First, autoboxing/unboxing greatly simplifies and streamlines code that requires object representations of a Java primitive type, such as **int** or **char**. Because such situations are found frequently in Java code, the benefits of autoboxing/unboxing affect nearly all Java programmers. Second, autoboxing/unboxing contributes greatly to the usability of another new feature: generics. Therefore, an understanding of autoboxing and auto-unboxing is needed before generics are examined. Third, autoboxing/unboxing subtly changes the way we think about the relationship between objects and the primitive types. These changes are more profound than the conceptual simplicity of these two features might at first suggest. Their effects are widely felt throughout the Java language.

Autoboxing and auto-unboxing are directly related to Java's type wrappers, and to the way that values are moved into and moved out of an instance of a wrapper. For this reason, we will begin with a brief review of the type wrappers and the process of boxing and unboxing values.

A Review of Type Wrappers and Boxing

As you know, Java uses primitive types (also called simple types), such as **int** or **double,** to hold the basic data types supported by the language. Primitive types, rather than objects, are used for these quantities for the sake of performance. Using objects for these values would add an unacceptable overhead to even the simplest of calculations. Thus, the primitive types are not part of the object hierarchy and they do not inherit **Object**.

Despite the performance benefit offered by the primitive types, there are times when you will need an object representation. For example, you can't pass a primitive type by reference to a method. Also, many of the standard data structures implemented by Java operate on objects, which means that you can't use these data structures to store primitive types. To handle these (and other) situations, Java provides *type wrappers,* which are classes that encapsulate a primitive type within an object. The type wrapper classes are shown here:

Boolean	Byte	Character	Double
Float	Long	Integer	Short

A primitive value is encapsulated within a wrapper when an object is constructed. Once encapsulated, the value can be obtained by calling any one of a number of methods defined by the wrapper. For example, all of the numeric wrappers offer the following methods:

byte byteValue( )	double doubleValue( )	float floatValue( )
int intValue( )	long longValue( )	short shortValue( )

Each method returns the value of the indicated primitive type. For example, an object of type **Long** can return its value as any of the built-in numeric types, including **short**, **double**, or **long**.

The process of encapsulating a value within an object is called *boxing*. Prior to Java 2, v5.0, all boxing took place manually, with the programmer explicitly constructing an instance of a wrapper with the desired value. For example, this line manually boxes the value 100 into an **Integer**:

```
Integer iOb = new Integer(100);
```

In this example, a new **Integer** object with the value 100 is explicitly created and a reference to this object is assigned to **iOb**.

The process of extracting a value from a type wrapper is called *unboxing*. Again, prior to Java 2, v5.0, all unboxing also took place manually, with the programmer explicitly calling a method on the wrapper to obtain its value. For example, this manually unboxes the value in **iOb** into an **int**:

```
int i = iOb.intValue();
```

Here, **intValue( )** returns the value encapsulated within **iOb** as an **int**. As explained earlier, other methods are available that return the wrapped value as a **byte**, **short**, **long**, **double**, or **float**. For example, to obtain the value in **iOb** as a **long**, you would call **iOb.longValue( )**. Thus, it is possible to unbox a value into a primitive type that differs from that of the type wrapper.

The same general procedure used by the preceding examples to manually box and unbox values has been employed since the original version of Java. Although this approach to boxing and unboxing works, it is both tedious and error-prone because it requires the programmer to manually create the appropriate object to wrap a value, and to explicitly obtain the proper primitive type when its value is needed. Fortunately, Java 2, v5.0 fundamentally improves on these essential procedures with the addition of autoboxing/unboxing.

Autoboxing/Unboxing Fundamentals

Autoboxing is the process by which a simple type, such as **int** or **double**, is automatically encapsulated (boxed) into its equivalent type wrapper whenever an object of that type is needed. There is no need to explicitly construct an object. Auto-unboxing is the process by which the value of a boxed object is automatically extracted (unboxed) from a type wrapper when its value is needed. There is no need to call a method such as **intValue( )** or **doubleValue( )**.

The addition of autoboxing and auto-unboxing greatly streamlines the coding of several algorithms, removing the tedium of manually boxing and unboxing values. It also helps prevent errors by eliminating the possibility of manually extracting the wrong type from a wrapper. Autoboxing also improves the use of generics and makes storing primitive types in a collection much easier.

With autoboxing it is no longer necessary to manually construct an object in order to wrap a primitive type. You need only assign that value to a type-wrapper reference. Java automatically constructs the object for you. For example, here is the modern way to construct an **Integer** object that has the value 100:

```
Integer iOb = 100; // autobox an int
```

Notice that no object is explicitly created through the use of **new**. Java handles this for you, automatically.

To unbox an object, simply assign that object reference to a variable of its corresponding primitive type. For example, to unbox **iOb**, you can use this line:

```
int i = iOb; // auto-unbox
```

Java handles the details for you.

Here is a short program that assembles the preceding pieces and demonstrates the basics of autoboxing/unboxing.

```
// Demonstrate autoboxing/unboxing.
class AutoBox {
  public static void main(String args[]) {

    Integer iOb = 100; // autobox an int

    int i = iOb; // auto-unbox
```

```
    System.out.println(i + " " + iOb);  // displays 100 100
  }
}
```

Again, notice that no **Integer** object need be explicitly created to box the value 100, nor is a call to **intValue( )** needed to unbox the value.

Autoboxing and Methods

In addition to the simple case of assignments, autoboxing automatically occurs whenever a primitive type must be converted into an object, and auto-unboxing takes place whenever an object must be converted into a primitive type. Thus, autoboxing/unboxing might occur when an argument is passed to a method, or when a value is returned by a method. For example, consider this example:

```
// Autoboxing/unboxing takes place with
// method parameters and return values.

class AutoBox2 {
  // Take an Integer parameter and return
  // an int value;
  static int m(Integer v) {
    return v ; // auto-unbox to int
  }

  public static void main(String args[]) {
    // Pass an int to m() and assign the return value
    // to an Integer.  Here, the argument 100 is autoboxed
    // into an Integer.  The return value is also autoboxed
    // into an Integer.
    Integer iOb = m(100);

    System.out.println(iOb);
  }
}
```

This program displays the following expected result:

```
100
```

In the program, notice that **m( )** specifies an **Integer** parameter and returns an **int** result. Inside **main( )**, **m( )** is passed the value 100. Because **m( )** is expecting an **Integer**, this value is automatically boxed. Then, **m( )** returns the **int** equivalent of its argument. This causes **v** to be auto-unboxed. Next, this **int** value is assigned to **iOb** in **main( )**, which causes the **int** return value to be autoboxed. The key point is that all of the transformations occur automatically.

Autoboxing/Unboxing Occurs in Expressions

In general, autoboxing/unboxing takes place whenever a conversion into an object or from an object is required. This applies to expressions. Within an expression, a numeric object is automatically unboxed. The outcome of the expression is reboxed, if necessary. For example, consider the following program:

```
// Autoboxing/unboxing occurs inside expressions.

class AutoBox3 {
  public static void main(String args[]) {

    Integer iOb, iOb2;
    int i;

    iOb = 100;
    System.out.println("Original value of iOb: " + iOb);

    // The following automatically unboxes iOb,
    // performs the increment, and then reboxes
    // the result back into iOb.
    ++iOb;
    System.out.println("After ++iOb: " + iOb);

    // Here, iOb is unboxed, the expression is
    // evaluated, and the result is reboxed and
    // assigned to iOb2.
    iOb2 = iOb + (iOb / 3);
    System.out.println("iOb2 after expression: " + iOb2);

    // The same expression is evaluated, but the
```

```
    // result is not reboxed.
    i = iOb + (iOb / 3);
    System.out.println("i after expression: " + i);

  }
}
```

The output is shown here:

```
Original value of iOb: 100
After ++iOb: 101
iOb2 after expression: 134
i after expression: 134
```

In the program, pay special attention to this line:

```
++iOb;
```

This causes the value in **iOb** to be incremented. It works like this: **iOb** is unboxed, the value is incremented, and the result is reboxed.

Auto-unboxing also allows you to mix different types of numeric objects in an expression. Once the values are unboxed, the standard type promotions and conversions are applied. For example, the following program is perfectly valid:

```
class AutoBox4 {
  public static void main(String args[]) {

    Integer iOb = 100;;
    Double dOb = 98.6;


    dOb = dOb + iOb;
    System.out.println("dOb after expression: " + dOb);
  }
}
```

The output is shown here:

```
dOb after expression: 198.6
```

As you can see, both the **Double** object **dOb** and the **Integer** object **iOb** participated in the addition and the result was reboxed and stored in **dOb**.

Because of auto-unboxing, you can use an integer numeric object to control a **switch** statement. For example, consider this fragment:

```
Integer iOb = 2;

switch(iOb) {
  case 1: System.out.println("one");
    break;
  case 2: System.out.println("two");
    break;
  default: System.out.println("error");
}
```

When the **switch** expression is evaluated, **iOb** is unboxed and its **int** value is obtained.

As the examples in the program show, because of autoboxing/unboxing, using numeric objects in an expression is both intuitive and easy. In the past, such code would have involved calls to methods such as **intValue( )**.

Autoboxing/Unboxing Boolean and Character Values

In addition to the numeric type wrappers, Java also supplies wrappers for **boolean** and **char**. These are **Boolean** and **Character**. Autoboxing/unboxing applies to these wrappers, too. For example, consider the following program:

```
// Autoboxing/unboxing a Boolean and Character.

class AutoBox5 {
  public static void main(String args[]) {

    // Autobox/unbox a boolean.
    Boolean b = true;

    // Below, b is auto-unboxed when used in
    // a conditional expression, such as an if.
    if(b) System.out.println("b is true");
```

```
    // Autobox/unbox a char.
    Character ch = 'x'; // box a char
    char ch2 = ch; // unbox a char

    System.out.println("ch2 is " + ch2);
  }
}
```

The output is shown here:

```
b is true
ch2 is x
```

The most important thing to notice about this program is the auto-unboxing of **b** inside the **if** conditional expression. As you should recall, the conditional expression that controls an **if** must evaluate to type **boolean**. Because of auto-unboxing, the **boolean** value contained within **b** is automatically unboxed when the conditional expression is evaluated. Thus, with the advent of Java 2, v5.0, a **Boolean** object can be used to control an **if** statement.

Because of auto-unboxing, a **Boolean** object can now also be used to control any of Java's loop statements. When a **Boolean** is used as the conditional expression in a **while**, **for**, or **do/while**, it is automatically unboxed into its **boolean** equivalent. For example, this is now perfectly valid code:

```
Boolean b;
// ...
while(b) { // ...
```

Autoboxing/Unboxing Helps Prevent Errors

In addition to the convenience that it offers, autoboxing/unboxing can also help prevent errors. For example, consider the following program:

```
// An error produced by manual unboxing.
class UnboxingError {
  public static void main(String args[]) {

    Integer iOb = 1000; // autobox the value 1000
```

```
    int i = iOb.byteValue(); // manually unbox as byte !!!

    System.out.println(i);  // does not display 1000 !
  }
}
```

This program displays not the expected value of 1000, but –24! The reason is that the value inside **iOb** is manually unboxed by calling **byteValue( )**, which causes the truncation of the value stored in **iOb**, which is 1000. This results in the garbage value of –24 being assigned to **i**. Auto-unboxing prevents this type of error because the value in **iOb** will always auto-unbox into a value compatible with **int**.

In general, because autoboxing always creates the proper object, and auto-unboxing always produces the proper value, there is no way for the process to produce the wrong type of object or value. In the rare instances where you want a type different than that produced by the automated process, you can still manually box and unbox values just as you have in the past. Of course, the benefits of autoboxing/unboxing are lost. In general, new code should employ autoboxing/unboxing. It is the way that modern Java code will be written.

A Word of Warning

Now that Java includes autoboxing and auto-unboxing, one might be tempted to use objects such as **Integer** or **Double** exclusively, abandoning primitives altogether. For example, with autoboxing/unboxing, it is possible to write code like this:

```
// A bad use of autoboxing/unboxing!
Double a, b, c;

a = 10.0;
b = 4.0;

c = Math.sqrt(a*a + b*b);

System.out.println("Hypotenuse is " + c);
```

In this example, objects of type **Double** hold values that are used to calculate the hypotenuse of a right triangle. Although this code is technically correct and does, in fact, work properly, it is a very bad use of autoboxing/unboxing. It is far less efficient than the equivalent code written using the primitive type **double**. The reason is that each autobox and auto-unbox adds overhead that is not present if the primitive type is used.

In general, you should restrict your use of the type wrappers to only those cases in which an object representation of a primitive type is required. Autoboxing/unboxing was not added to Java as a "back door" way of eliminating the primitive types.

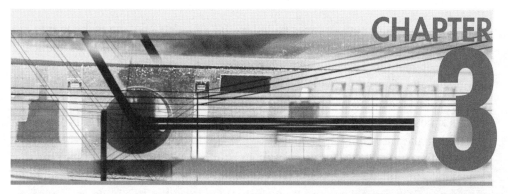

CHAPTER 3

Generics

Of the many new features added by Java 2, v5.0, the one that has the most profound impact is *generics*. Not only did it add a new syntactical element to Java, it also caused changes to many of the classes and methods in the core API. Through the use of generics, it is possible to create classes, interfaces, and methods that will work in a type-safe manner with various kinds of data. Many algorithms are logically the same no matter what type of data they are being applied to. For example, the mechanism that supports a stack is the same whether that stack is storing items of type **Integer**, **String**, **Object**, or **Thread**. With generics, you can define an algorithm once, independently of any specific type of data, and then apply that algorithm to a wide variety of data types without any additional effort. The expressive power generics add to the language profoundly changes the way that Java code is written.

Perhaps the one feature of Java that has been most significantly impacted by generics is the Collections Framework. As you know, the Collections Framework defines several classes, such as lists and maps, that manage collections. The collection classes have always been able to work with any type of object. The benefit that generics add is that the collection classes can now be used with complete type safety. Thus, in addition to providing a powerful, new language element, generics also enabled an existing feature to be substantially improved. This is why generics represent such an important addition to Java.

What Are Generics?

At its core, the term *generics* means *parameterized types*. Parameterized types are important because they enable you to create classes, interfaces, and methods in which the type of data upon which they operate is specified as a parameter. Using generics, it is possible to create a single class, for example, that automatically works with different types of data. A class, interface, or method that operates on a parameterized type is called *generic,* as in *generic class* or *generic method*.

It is important to understand that Java has always given you the ability to create generalized classes, interfaces, and methods by operating through references of type **Object**. Because **Object** is the superclass of all other classes, an **Object** reference can refer to any type object. Thus, in pre-generics code, generalized classes, interfaces, and methods used **Object** references to operate on various types of objects. The problem was that they could not do so with type safety.

Generics add the type safety that was lacking. They also streamline the process because it is no longer necessary to explicitly employ casts to translate between **Object** and the type of data that is actually being operated upon. With generics, all casts are automatic and implicit. Thus, generics expand your ability to reuse code, and let you do so safely and easily.

CAUTION

A warning to C++ programmers: Although generics are similar to templates in C++, they are not the same. There are some fundamental differences between the two approaches to generic types. If you have a background in C++, it is important to not jump to conclusions about how generics work in Java.

A Simple Generics Example

Let's begin with a simple example of a generic class. The following program defines two classes. The first is the generic class **Gen**, and the second is **GenDemo**, which uses **Gen**.

```
// A simple generic class.
// Here, T is a type parameter that
// will be replaced by a real type
// when an object of type Gen is created.
class Gen<T> {
  T ob; // declare an object of type T

  // Pass the constructor a reference to
  // an object of type T.
  Gen(T o) {
    ob = o;
  }

  // Return ob.
  T getob() {
    return ob;
  }
```

```
  // Show type of T.
  void showType() {
    System.out.println("Type of T is " +
                         ob.getClass().getName());
  }
}

// Demonstrate the generic class.
class GenDemo {
  public static void main(String args[]) {
    // Create a Gen reference for Integers.
    Gen<Integer> iOb;

    // Create a Gen<Integer> object and assign its
    // reference to iOb.  Notice the use of autoboxing
    // to encapsulate the value 88 within an Integer object.
    iOb = new Gen<Integer>(88);

    // Show the type of data used by iOb.
    iOb.showType();

    // Get the value of iOb. Notice that
    // no cast is needed.
    int v = iOb.getob();
    System.out.println("value: " + v);

    System.out.println();

    // Create a Gen object for Strings.
    Gen<String> strOb = new Gen<String>("Generics Test");

    // Show the type of data used by strOb.
    strOb.showType();

    // Get the value of strOb. Again, notice
    // that no cast is needed.
    String str = strOb.getob();
    System.out.println("value: " + str);
  }
}
```

The output produced by the program is shown here:

```
Type of T is java.lang.Integer
value: 88

Type of T is java.lang.String
value: Generics Test
```

Let's examine this program carefully.

First, notice how **Gen** is declared by the following line:

```
class Gen<T> {
```

Here, **T** is the name of a *type parameter.* This name is used as a placeholder for the actual type that will be passed to **Gen** when an object is created. Thus, **T** is used within **Gen** whenever the type parameter is needed. Notice that **T** is contained within < >. This syntax can be generalized. Whenever a type parameter is being declared, it is specified within angle brackets. Because **Gen** uses a type parameter, **Gen** is a generic class, which is also called a *parameterized type.*

Next, **T** is used to declare an object called **ob**, as shown here:

```
T ob; // declare an object of type T
```

As explained, **T** is a placeholder for the actual type that will be specified when a **Gen** object is created. Thus, **ob** will be an object of the type passed to **T**. For example, if type **String** is passed to **T**, then in that instance, **ob** will be of type **String**.

Now consider **Gen**'s constructor:

```
Gen(T o) {
  ob = o;
}
```

Notice that its parameter, **o**, is of type **T**. This means that the actual type of **o** is determined by the type passed to **T** when a **Gen** object is created. Also, because both the parameter **o** and the member variable **ob** are of type **T**, they will both be of the same actual type when a **Gen** object is created.

The type parameter **T** can also be used to specify the return type of a method, as is the case with the **getob( )** method, shown here:

```
T getob() {
  return ob;
}
```

Because **ob** is also of the type **T**, its type is compatible with the return type specified by **getob( )**.

The **showType( )** method displays the type of **T** by calling **getName( )** on the **Class** object returned by the call to **getClass( )** on **ob**. The **getClass( )** method is defined by **Object**, and is thus a member of all class types. It returns a **Class** object that corresponds to the type of the class of the object on which it is called. **Class** defines the **getName( )** method, which returns a string representation of the class name.

The **GenDemo** class demonstrates the generic **Gen** class. It first creates a version of **Gen** for integers, as shown here:

```
Gen<Integer> iOb;
```

Look closely at this declaration. First, notice that the type **Integer** is specified within the angle brackets after **Gen**. In this case, **Integer** is a *type argument* that is passed to **Gen**'s type parameter, **T**. This effectively creates a version of **Gen** in which all references to **T** are translated into references to **Integer**. Thus, for this declaration, **ob** is of type **Integer**, and the return type of **getob( )** is of type **Integer**.

Before moving on, it's necessary to state that the Java compiler does not actually create different versions of **Gen**, or of any other generic class. Although it's helpful to think in these terms, it is not what actually happens. Instead, the compiler removes all generic type information, substituting the necessary casts, to make your code *behave as if* a specific version of **Gen** was created. Thus, there is really only one version of **Gen** that actually exists in your program. The process of removing generic type information is called *erasure,* and we will return to this topic later in this chapter.

The next line assigns to **iOb** a reference to an instance of an **Integer** version of the **Gen** class:

```
iOb = new Gen<Integer>(88);
```

Notice that when the **Gen** constructor is called, the type argument **Integer** is also specified. This is necessary because the type of the object (in this case **iOb**) to which the reference is being assigned is of type **Gen<Integer>**. Thus, the reference returned by **new** must also be of type **Gen<Integer>**. If it isn't, a compile-time error will result. For example, the following assignment will cause a compile-time error:

```
iOb = new Gen<Double>(88.0); // Error!
```

Because **iOb** is of type **Gen<Integer>**, it can't be used to refer to an object of **Gen<Double>**. This type checking is one of the main benefits of generics because it ensures type safety.

As the comments in the program state, the assignment

```
iOb = new Gen<Integer>(88);
```

makes use of autoboxing to encapsulate the value 88, which is an **int**, into an **Integer**. This works because **Gen<Integer>** creates a constructor that takes an **Integer** argument. Because an **Integer** is expected, Java will automatically box 88 inside one. Of course, the assignment could also have been written explicitly, like this:

```
iOb = new Gen<Integer>(new Integer(88));
```

However, there would be no benefit to using this version.

The program then displays the type of **ob** within **iOb**, which is **Integer**. Next, the program obtains the value of **ob** by use of the following line:

```
int v = iOb.getob();
```

Because the return type of **getob( )** is **T**, which was replaced by **Integer** when **iOb** was declared, the return type of **getob( )** is also **Integer**, which unboxes into **int** when assigned to **v** (which is an **int**). Thus, there is no need to cast the return type of **getob( )** to **Integer**. Of course, it's not necessary to use the auto-unboxing feature. The preceding line could have been written like this, too:

```
int v = iOb.getob().intValue();
```

However, the auto-unboxing feature makes the code more compact.

Next, **GenDemo** declares an object of type **Gen<String>**:

```
Gen<String> strOb = new Gen<String>("Generics Test");
```

Because the type argument is **String**, **String** is substituted for **T** inside **Gen**. This creates (conceptually) a **String** version of **Gen**, as the remaining lines in the program demonstrate.

Generics Work Only with Objects

When declaring an instance of a generic type, the type argument passed to the type parameter must be a class type. You cannot use a primitive type, such as **int** or **char**. For example, with **Gen**, it is possible to pass any class type to **T**, but you cannot pass a primitive type to a type parameter. Therefore, the following declaration is illegal:

```
Gen<int> strOb = new Gen<int>(53); // Error, can't use primitive type
```

Of course, not being able to specify a primitive type is not a serious restriction, because you can use the type wrappers (as the preceding example did) to encapsulate a primitive type. Further, Java's autoboxing and auto-unboxing mechanism makes the use of the type wrapper transparent.

Generic Types Differ Based on Their Type Arguments

A key point to understand about generic types is that a reference of one specific version of a generic type is not type-compatible with another version of the same generic type. For example, assuming the program just shown, the following line of code is in error, and will not compile:

```
iOb = strOb; // Wrong!
```

Even though both **iOb** and **strOb** are of type **Gen<T>**, they are references to different types because their type parameters differ. This is part of the way that generics add type safety and prevent errors.

y

elf the following question: Given that
ric **Gen** class can be achieved without
s the data type and employing the proper
generic? The answer is that generics
operations involving **Gen**. In the process,
sts and type-check code by hand.
, first consider the following program
en:

: to Gen

ject

```
    // Pass the constructor a reference to
    // an object of type Object
    NonGen(Object o) {
      ob = o;
    }

    // Return type Object.
    Object getob() {
      return ob;
    }

    // Show type of ob.
    void showType() {
      System.out.println("Type of ob is " +
                    ob.getClass().getName());
    }
  }

// Demonstrate the non-generic class.
class NonGenDemo {
  public static void main(String args[]) {
    NonGen iOb;

    // Create NonGen Object and store
```

```
      // an Integer in it. Autoboxing still occurs.
      iOb = new NonGen(88);

      // Show the type of data used by iOb.
      iOb.showType();

      // Get the value of iOb.
      // This time, a cast is necessary.
      int v = (Integer) iOb.getob();
      System.out.println("value: " + v);

      System.out.println();

      // Create another NonGen object and
      // store a String in it.
      NonGen strOb = new NonGen("Non-Generics Test");

      // Show the type of data used by strOb.
      strOb.showType();

      // Get the value of strOb.
      // Again, notice that a cast is necessary.
      String str = (String) strOb.getob();
      System.out.println("value: " + str);

      // This compiles, but is conceptually wrong!
      iOb = strOb;
      v = (Integer) iOb.getob(); // run-time error!
   }
}
```

There are several things of interest in this version. First, notice that **NonGen** replaces all uses of **T** with **Object**. This makes **NonGen** able to store any type of object, as can the generic version. However, it also prevents the Java compiler from having any real knowledge about the type of data actually stored in **NonGen**, which is bad for two reasons. First, explicit casts must be employed to retrieve the stored data. Second, many kinds of type mismatch errors cannot be found until run time. Let's look closely at each problem.

Notice this line:

```
int v = (Integer) iOb.getob();
```

Because the return type of **getob( )** is **Object**, the cast to **Integer** is necessary to enable that value to be auto-unboxed and stored in **v**. If you remove the cast, the program will not compile. With the generic version, this cast was implicit. In the nongeneric version, the cast must be explicit. This is not only an inconvenience, but a potential source of error.

Now, consider the following sequence from near the end of the program:

```
// This compiles, but is conceptually wrong!
iOb = strOb;
v = (Integer) iOb.getob(); // runtime error!
```

Here, **strOb** is assigned to **iOb**. However, **strOb** refers to an object that contains a string, not an integer. This assignment is syntactically valid because all **NonGen** references are the same, and any **NonGen** reference can refer to any other **NonGen** object. However, the statement is semantically wrong, as the next line shows. Here, the return type of **getob( )** is cast to **Integer** and then an attempt is made to assign this value to **v**. The trouble is that **iOb** now refers to an object that stores a **String**, not an **Integer**. Unfortunately, without use of generics, the Java compiler has no way to know this. Instead, a run-time exception occurs when the cast to **Integer** is attempted. As you know, it is extremely bad to have run-time exceptions occur in your code!

The preceding sequence can't occur when generics are used. If this sequence were attempted in the generic version of the program, the compiler would catch it and report an error, thus preventing a serious bug that results in a run-time exception. The ability to create type-safe code in which type-mismatch errors are caught at compile time is a key advantage of generics. Although using **Object** references to create "generic" code has always been possible, that code was not type-safe and its misuse could result in run-time exceptions. Generics prevent this from occurring. In essence, through generics, what were once run-time errors have become compile-time errors. This is a major advantage.

A Generic Class with Two Type Parameters

You can declare more than one type parameter in a generic type. To specify two or more type parameters, simply use a comma-separated list. For example, the following **TwoGen** class is a variation of the **Gen** class that has two type parameters:

```
// A simple generic class with two type
// parameters: T and V.
class TwoGen<T, V> {
  T ob1;
  V ob2;

  // Pass the constructor a reference to
  // an object of type T.
  TwoGen(T o1, V o2) {
    ob1 = o1;
    ob2 = o2;
  }

  // Show types of T and V.
  void showTypes() {
    System.out.println("Type of T is " +
                       ob1.getClass().getName());

    System.out.println("Type of V is " +
                       ob2.getClass().getName());
  }

  T getob1() {
    return ob1;
  }

  V getob2() {
    return ob2;
  }
}

// Demonstrate TwoGen.
class SimpGen {
  public static void main(String args[]) {

    TwoGen<Integer, String> tgObj =
      new TwoGen<Integer, String>(88, "Generics");
```

```
      // Show the types.
      tgObj.showTypes();

      // Obtain and show values.
      int v = tgObj.getob1();
      System.out.println("value: " + v);

      String str = tgObj.getob2();
      System.out.println("value: " + str);
   }
}
```

The output from this program is shown here:

```
Type of T is java.lang.Integer
Type of V is java.lang.String
value: 88
value: Generics
```

Notice how **TwoGen** is declared:

```
class TwoGen<T, V> {
```

It specifies two type parameters, **T** and **V**, separated by a comma. Because it has two type parameters, two type arguments must be passed to **TwoGen** when an object is created, as shown next:

```
TwoGen<Integer, String> tgObj =
  new TwoGen<Integer, String>(88, "Generics");
```

In this case, **Integer** is substituted for **T** and **String** is substituted for **V**.

Although the two type arguments differ in this example, it is possible for both types to be the same. For example, the following line of code is valid:

```
TwoGen<String, String> x = new TwoGen<String, String>("A", "B");
```

In this case, both **T** and **V** would be of type **String**. Of course, if the type arguments were always the same, then two type parameters would be unnecessary.

The General Form of a Generic Class

The generics syntax shown in the preceding examples can be generalized. Here is the syntax for declaring a generic class:

> class *class-name<type-param-list>* { // ...

Here is the syntax for declaring a reference to a generics class:

> class *class-name<type-arg-list> var-name* =
>   new *class-name<type-arg-list>(cons-arg-list)*;

Bounded Types

In the preceding examples, the type parameters could be replaced by any class type. This is fine for many purposes, but sometimes it is useful to limit the types that can be passed to a type parameter. For example, assume that you want to create a generic class that contains a method that returns the average of an array of numbers. Furthermore, you want to use the class to obtain the average of an array of any type of number, including integers, floats, and doubles. Thus, you want to specify the type of the numbers generically, using a type parameter. To create such a class, you might try something like this:

```
// Stats attempts (unsuccessfully) to
// create a generic class that can compute
// the average of an array of numbers of
// any given type.
//
// The class contains an error!
class Stats<T> {
  T[] nums; // nums is an array of type T

  // Pass the constructor a reference to
  // an array of type T.
  Stats(T[] o) {
    nums = o;
  }

  // Return type double in all cases.
  double average() {
    double sum = 0.0;
```

```
     for(int i=0; i < nums.length; i++)
       sum += nums[i].doubleValue(); // Error!!!

     return sum / nums.length;
   }
}
```

In **Stats**, the **average( )** method attempts to obtain the **double** version of each number in the **nums** array by calling **doubleValue( )**. Because all numeric classes, such as **Integer** and **Double**, are subclasses of **Number**, and **Number** defines the **doubleValue( )** method, this method is available to all numeric wrapper classes. The trouble is that the compiler has no way to know that you are intending to create **Stats** objects using only numeric types. Thus, when you try to compile **Stats**, an error is reported that indicates that the **doubleValue( )** method is unknown. To solve this problem, you need some way to tell the compiler that you intend to pass only numeric types to **T**. Furthermore, you need some way to *ensure* that *only* numeric types are actually passed.

To handle such situations, Java provides *bounded types*. When specifying a type parameter, you can create an upper bound that declares the superclass from which all type arguments must be derived. This is accomplished through the use of an **extends** clause when specifying the type parameter, as shown here:

<*T* extends *superclass*>

This specifies that *T* can only be replaced by *superclass*, or subclasses of *superclass*. Thus, *superclass* defines an inclusive, upper limit.

You can use an upper bound to fix the **Stats** class shown earlier by specifying **Number** as an upper bound, as shown here:

```
// In this version of Stats, the type argument for
// T must be either Number, or a class derived
// from Number.
class Stats<T extends Number> {
  T[] nums; // array of Number or subclass

  // Pass the constructor a reference to
  // an array of type Number or subclass.
  Stats(T[] o) {
    nums = o;
  }
```

```
      // Return type double in all cases.
      double average() {
        double sum = 0.0;

        for(int i=0; i < nums.length; i++)
          sum += nums[i].doubleValue();

        return sum / nums.length;
      }
    }

    // Demonstrate Stats.
    class BoundsDemo {
      public static void main(String args[]) {

        Integer inums[] = { 1, 2, 3, 4, 5 };
        Stats<Integer> iob = new Stats<Integer>(inums);
        double v = iob.average();
        System.out.println("iob average is " + v);

        Double dnums[] = { 1.1, 2.2, 3.3, 4.4, 5.5 };
        Stats<Double> dob = new Stats<Double>(dnums);
        double w = dob.average();
        System.out.println("dob average is " + w);

        // This won't compile because String is not a
        // subclass of Number.
    //    String strs[] = { "1", "2", "3", "4", "5" };
    //    Stats<String> strob = new Stats<String>(strs);

    //    double x = strob.average();
    //    System.out.println("strob average is " + v);

      }
    }
```

The output is shown here:

```
Average is 3.0
Average is 3.3
```

Notice how **Stats** is now declared by this line:

```
class Stats<T extends Number> {
```

Because the type **T** is now bounded by **Number**, the Java compiler knows that all objects of type **T** can call **doubleValue( )** because it is a method declared by **Number**. This is, by itself, a major advantage. However, as an added bonus, the bounding of **T** also prevents nonnumeric **Stats** objects from being created. For example, if you try removing the comments from the lines at the end of the program, and then try recompiling, you will receive compile-time errors because **String** is not a subclass of **Number**.

Using Wildcard Arguments

As useful as type safety is, sometimes it can get in the way of perfectly acceptable constructs. For example, given the **Stats** class shown at the end of the preceding section, assume that you want to add a method called **sameAvg( )** that determines if two **Stats** objects contain arrays that yield the same average, no matter what type of numeric data each object holds. For example, if one object contains the **double** values 1.0, 2.0, and 3.0, and the other object contains the integer values 2, 1, and 3, then the averages will be the same. One way to implement **sameAvg( )** is to pass it a **Stats** argument, and then compare the average of that argument against the invoking object, returning true only if the averages are the same. For example, you want to be able to call **sameAvg( )** as shown here:

```
Integer inums[] = { 1, 2, 3, 4, 5 };
Double dnums[] = { 1.1, 2.2, 3.3, 4.4, 5.5 };

Stats<Integer> iob = new Stats<Integer>(inums);
Stats<Double> dob = new Stats<Double>(dnums);

if(iob.sameAvg(dob))
  System.out.println("Averages are the same.");
else
  System.out.println("Averages differ.");
```

Because **Stats** is generic and its **average( )** method can work on any type of **Stats** object, it seems that creating **sameAvg( )** would be straightforward. Unfortunately, trouble starts as soon as you try to declare a parameter of type **Stats**. Because **Stats** is a parameterized type, what do you specify for **Stats'** type parameter when you declare a parameter of that type?

You might think of a solution like this, in which **T** is used as the type parameter:

```
// This won't work!
// Determine if two averages are the same.
boolean sameAvg(Stats<T> ob) {
  if(average() == ob.average())
    return true;

  return false;
}
```

The trouble with this attempt is that it will work only with other **Stats** objects whose type is the same as the invoking object. For example, if the invoking object is of type **Stats<Integer>**, then the parameter **ob** must also be of type **Stats<Integer>**. It can't be used to compare the average of an object of type **Stats<Double>** with the average of an object of type **Stats<Short>**, for example. Therefore, this approach won't work except in a very narrow context and does not yield a general (i.e., generic) solution.

To create a generic **sameAvg( )** method, you must use another feature of Java generics: the *wildcard* argument. The wildcard argument is specified by the **?**, and it represents an unknown type. Using a wildcard, here is one way to write the **sameAvg( )** method:

```
// Determine if two averages are the same.
// Notice the use of the wildcard.
boolean sameAvg(Stats<?> ob) {
  if(average() == ob.average())
    return true;

  return false;
}
```

Here, **Stats<?>** matches any **Stats** object, allowing any two **Stats** objects to have their averages compared. The following program demonstrates this:

```
// Use a wildcard.
class Stats<T extends Number> {
  T[] nums; // array of Number or subclass

  // Pass the constructor a reference to
  // an array of type Number or subclass.
```

```
  Stats(T[] o) {
    nums = o;
  }

  // Return type double in all cases.
  double average() {
    double sum = 0.0;

    for(int i=0; i < nums.length; i++)
      sum += nums[i].doubleValue();

    return sum / nums.length;
  }

  // Determine if two averages are the same.
  // Notice the use of the wildcard.
  boolean sameAvg(Stats<?> ob) {
    if(average() == ob.average())
      return true;

    return false;
  }
}

// Demonstrate wildcard.
class WildcardDemo {
  public static void main(String args[]) {
    Integer inums[] = { 1, 2, 3, 4, 5 };
    Stats<Integer> iob = new Stats<Integer>(inums);
    double v = iob.average();
    System.out.println("iob average is " + v);

    Double dnums[] = { 1.1, 2.2, 3.3, 4.4, 5.5 };
    Stats<Double> dob = new Stats<Double>(dnums);
    double w = dob.average();
    System.out.println("dob average is " + w);

    Float fnums[] = { 1.0F, 2.0F, 3.0F, 4.0F, 5.0F };
    Stats<Float> fob = new Stats<Float>(fnums);
    double x = fob.average();
    System.out.println("fob average is " + x);

    // See which arrays have same average.
    System.out.print("Averages of iob and dob ");
```

```
   if(iob.sameAvg(dob))
     System.out.println("are the same.");
   else
     System.out.println("differ.");

   System.out.print("Averages of iob and fob ");
   if(iob.sameAvg(fob))
     System.out.println("are the same.");
   else
     System.out.println("differ.");
 }
}
```

The output is shown here:

```
iob average is 3.0
dob average is 3.3
fob average is 3.0
Averages of iob and dob differ.
Averages of iob and fob are the same.
```

One last point: It is important to understand that the wildcard does not affect what type of **Stats** objects can be created. This is governed by the **extends** clause in the **Stats** declaration. The wildcard simply matches any *valid* **Stats** object.

Bounded Wildcards

Wildcard arguments can be bounded in much the same way that a type parameter can be bounded. A bounded wildcard is especially important when you are creating a generic type that will operate on a class hierarchy. To understand why, let's work through an example. Consider the following hierarchy of classes that encapsulates coordinates:

```
// Two-dimensional coordinates.
class TwoD {
  int x, y;

  TwoD(int a, int b) {
    x = a;
    y = b;
```

```
    }
}

// Three-dimensional coordinates.
class ThreeD extends TwoD {
  int z;

  ThreeD(int a, int b, int c) {
    super(a, b);
    z = c;
  }
}

// Four-dimensional coordinates.
class FourD extends ThreeD {
  int t;

  FourD(int a, int b, int c, int d) {
    super(a, b, c);
    t = d;
  }
}
```

At the top of the hierarchy is **TwoD**, which encapsulates a two-dimensional, XY coordinate. **TwoD** is inherited by **ThreeD**, which adds a third dimension, creating an XYZ coordinate. **ThreeD** is inherited by **FourD**, which adds a fourth dimension (time), yielding a four-dimensional coordinate.

Shown next is a generic class called **Coords**, which stores an array of coordinates:

```
// This class holds an array of coordinate objects.
class Coords<T extends TwoD> {
  T[] coords;

  Coords(T[] o) { coords = o; }
}
```

Notice that **Coords** specifies a type parameter bounded by **TwoD**. This means that any array stored in a **Coords** object will contain objects of type **TwoD** or one of its subclasses.

Now, assume that you want to write a method that displays the X and Y coordinates for each element in the **coords** array of a **Coords** object. Because all types of **Coords** objects have at least two coordinates (X and Y), this is easy to do using a wildcard, as shown here:

```
static void showXY(Coords<?> c) {
  System.out.println("X Y Coordinates:");
  for(int i=0; i < c.coords.length; i++)
    System.out.println(c.coords[i].x + " " +
                       c.coords[i].y);
  System.out.println();
}
```

Because **Coords** is a bounded generic type that specifies **TwoD** as an upper bound, all objects that can be used to create a **Coords** object will be arrays of type **TwoD**, or of classes derived from **TwoD**. Thus, **showXY( )** can display the contents of any **Coords** object.

However, what if you want to create a method that displays the X, Y, and Z coordinates of a **ThreeD** or **FourD** object? The trouble is that not all **Coords** objects will have three coordinates, because a **Coords<TwoD>** object will only have X and Y. Therefore, how do you write a method that displays the X, Y, and Z coordinates for **Coords<ThreeD>** and **Coords<FourD>** objects, while preventing that method from being used with **Coords<TwoD>** objects? The answer is the *bounded wildcard argument.*

A bounded wildcard specifies either an upper bound or a lower bound for the type argument. This enables you to restrict the types of objects upon which a method will operate. The most common bounded wildcard is the upper bound, which is created using an **extends** clause in much the same way it is used to create a bounded type.

Using a bounded wildcard, it is easy to create a method that displays the X, Y, and Z coordinates of a **Coords** object, if that object actually has those three coordinates. For example, the following **showXYZ( )** method shows the X, Y, and Z coordinates of the elements stored in a **Coords** object, if those elements are actually of type **ThreeD** (or are derived from **ThreeD**):

```
static void showXYZ(Coords<? extends ThreeD> c) {
  System.out.println("X Y Z Coordinates:");
  for(int i=0; i < c.coords.length; i++)
```

```
      System.out.println(c.coords[i].x + " " +
                         c.coords[i].y + " " +
                         c.coords[i].z);
   System.out.println();
}
```

Notice that an **extends** clause has been added to the wildcard in the declaration
of parameter **c**. It states that the **?** can match any type as long as it is **ThreeD**,
or a class derived from **ThreeD**. Thus, the **extends** clause establishes an upper
bound that the **?** can match. Because of this bound, **showXYZ( )** can be called
with references to objects of type **Coords<ThreeD>** or **Coords<FourD>**, but
not with a reference of type **Coords<TwoD>**. Attempting to call **showXZY( )**
with a **Coords<TwoD>** reference results in a compile-time error, thus ensuring
type safety.

Here is an entire program that demonstrates the actions of a bounded wildcard
argument:

```
// Bounded Wildcard arguments.

// Two-dimensional coordinates.
class TwoD {
  int x, y;

  TwoD(int a, int b) {
    x = a;
    y = b;
  }
}

// Three-dimensional coordinates.
class ThreeD extends TwoD {
  int z;

  ThreeD(int a, int b, int c) {
    super(a, b);
    z = c;
  }
}

// Four-dimensional coordinates.
class FourD extends ThreeD {
  int t;
```

```
    FourD(int a, int b, int c, int d) {
      super(a, b, c);
      t = d;
    }
}

// This class holds an array of coordinate objects.
class Coords<T extends TwoD> {
  T[] coords;

  Coords(T[] o) { coords = o; }
}

// Demonstrate a bounded wildcard.
class BoundedWildcard {
  static void showXY(Coords<?> c) {
    System.out.println("X Y Coordinates:");
    for(int i=0; i < c.coords.length; i++)
      System.out.println(c.coords[i].x + " " +
                          c.coords[i].y);
    System.out.println();
  }

  static void showXYZ(Coords<? extends ThreeD> c) {
    System.out.println("X Y Z Coordinates:");
    for(int i=0; i < c.coords.length; i++)
      System.out.println(c.coords[i].x + " " +
                          c.coords[i].y + " " +
                          c.coords[i].z);
    System.out.println();
  }

  static void showAll(Coords<? extends FourD> c) {
    System.out.println("X Y Z T Coordinates:");
    for(int i=0; i < c.coords.length; i++)
      System.out.println(c.coords[i].x + " " +
                          c.coords[i].y + " " +
                          c.coords[i].z + " " +
                          c.coords[i].t);
    System.out.println();
  }

  public static void main(String args[]) {
    TwoD td[] = {
```

```
      new TwoD(0, 0),
      new TwoD(7, 9),
      new TwoD(18, 4),
      new TwoD(-1, -23)
    };

    Coords<TwoD> tdlocs = new Coords<TwoD>(td);

    System.out.println("Contents of tdlocs.");
    showXY(tdlocs); // OK, is a TwoD
//  showXYZ(tdlocs); // Error, not a ThreeD
//  showAll(tdlocs); // Error, not a FourD

    // Now, create some FourD objects.
    FourD fd[] = {
      new FourD(1, 2, 3, 4),
      new FourD(6, 8, 14, 8),
      new FourD(22, 9, 4, 9),
      new FourD(3, -2, -23, 17)
    };

    Coords<FourD> fdlocs = new Coords<FourD>(fd);

    System.out.println("Contents of fdlocs.");
    // These are all OK.
    showXY(fdlocs);
    showXYZ(fdlocs);
    showAll(fdlocs);
  }
}
```

The output from the program is shown here:

```
Contents of tdlocs.
X Y Coordinates:
0 0
7 9
18 4
-1 -23

Contents of fdlocs.
X Y Coordinates:
1 2
6 8
```

```
22 9
3 -2

X Y Z Coordinates:
1 2 3
6 8 14
22 9 4
3 -2 -23

X Y Z T Coordinates:
1 2 3 4
6 8 14 8
22 9 4 9
3 -2 -23 17
```

Notice these commented-out lines:

```
//   showXYZ(tdlocs); // Error, not a ThreeD
//   showAll(tdlocs); // Error, not a FourD
```

Because **tdlocs** is a **Coords(TwoD)** object, it cannot be used to called **showXYZ( )** or **showAll( )** because bounded wildcard arguments in their declarations prevent it. To prove this to yourself, try removing the comment symbols and then attempt to compile the program. You will receive compilation errors because of the type mismatches.

In general, to establish an upper bound for a wildcard, use the following type of wildcard expression:

<? extends *superclass*>

where *superclass* is the name of the class that serves as the upper bound. Remember, this is an inclusive clause, because the class forming the upper bound (that is, specified by *superclass*) is also within bounds.

You can also specify a lower bound for a wildcard by adding a **super** clause to a wildcard declaration. Here is its general form:

<? super *subclass*>

In this case, only classes that are superclasses of *subclass* are acceptable arguments. This is an exclusive clause, because it will not match the class specified by *subclass*.

Creating a Generic Method

As the preceding examples have shown, methods inside a generic class can make use of a class' type parameter and are, therefore, automatically generic relative to the type parameter. However, it is possible to declare a generic method that uses one or more type parameters of its own. Furthermore, it is possible to create a generic method that is enclosed within a nongeneric class.

Let's begin with an example. The following program declares a nongeneric class called **GenMethDemo** and a static generic method within that class called **isIn( )**. The **isIn( )** method determines if an object is a member of an array. It can be used with any type of object and array as long as the array contains objects that are compatible with the type of the object being sought.

```
// Demonstrate a simple generic method.
class GenMethDemo {

  // Determine if an object is in an array.
  static <T, V extends T> boolean isIn(T x, V[] y) {

    for(int i=0; i < y.length; i++)
      if(x.equals(y[i])) return true;

    return false;
  }

  public static void main(String args[]) {

    // Use isIn() on Integers.
    Integer nums[] = { 1, 2, 3, 4, 5 };

    if(isIn(2, nums))
      System.out.println("2 is in nums");

    if(!isIn(7, nums))
      System.out.println("7 is not in nums");

    System.out.println();

    // Use isIn() on Strings.
    String strs[] = { "one", "two", "three",
                      "four", "five" };
```

```
    if(isIn("two", strs))
      System.out.println("two is in strs");

    if(!isIn("seven", strs))
      System.out.println("seven is not in strs");

    // Opps! Won't compile! Types must be compatible.
//    if(isIn("two", nums))
//      System.out.println("two is in strs");
  }
}
```

The output from the program is shown here:

```
2 is in nums
7 is not in nums

two is in strs
seven is not in strs
```

Let's examine **isIn( )** closely. First, notice how it is declared by this line:

```
static <T, V extends T> boolean isIn(T x, V[] y) {
```

The type parameters are declared *before* the return type of the method. Second, notice that the type **V** is upper-bounded by **T**. Thus, **V** must be either the same as type **T** or a subclass of **T**. This relationship enforces that **isIn( )** can be called only with arguments that are compatible with each other. Also notice that **isIn( )** is static, enabling it to be called independently of any object. Understand, though, that generic methods can be either static or nonstatic. There is no restriction in this regard.

Now, notice how **isIn( )** is called within **main( )** by use of the normal call syntax, without the need to specify type arguments. This is because the types of the arguments are automatically discerned, and the types of **T** and **V** are adjusted accordingly. For example, in the first call

```
if(isIn(2, nums))
```

the type of the first argument is **Integer** (due to autoboxing), which causes **Integer** to be substituted for **T**. The base type of the second argument is also **Integer**, which makes **Integer** a substitute for **V**, too.

In the second call, **String** types are used, and the types of **T** and **V** are replaced by **String**.

Now, notice the commented-out code, shown here:

```
//    if(isIn("two", nums))
//      System.out.println("two is in strs");
```

If you remove the comments and then try to compile the program, you will receive an error. The reason is that the type parameter **V** is bounded by **T** in the **extends** clause in **V**'s declaration. This means that **V** must be either type **T** or a subclass of **T**. In this case, the first argument is of type **String**, making **T** into **String**, but the second argument is of type **Integer**, which is not a subclass of **String**. This causes a compile-time type-mismatch error. This ability to enforce type safety is one of the most important advantages of generic methods.

The syntax used to create **isIn( )** can be generalized. Here is the syntax for a generic method:

<type-param-list> ret-type meth-name(param-list) { // ...

In all cases, *type-param-list* is a comma-separated list of type parameters. Notice that for a generic method, the type parameter list precedes the return type.

Generic Constructors

It is also possible for constructors to be generic, even if their class is not. For example, consider the following short program:

```
// Use a generic constructor.
class GenCons {
  private double val;

  <T extends Number> GenCons(T arg) {
    val = arg.doubleValue();
  }

  void showval() {
    System.out.println("val: " + val);
  }
}
```

```
class GenConsDemo {
  public static void main(String args[]) {

    GenCons test = new GenCons(100);
    GenCons test2 = new GenCons(123.5F);

    test.showval();
    test2.showval();
  }
}
```

The output is shown here:

```
val: 100.0
val: 123.5
```

Because **GenCons( )** specifies a parameter of a generic type, which must be a subclass of **Number**, **GenCons( )** can be called with any numeric type, including **Integer**, **Float**, or **Double**. Therefore, even though **GenCons** is not a generic class, its constructor is generic.

Generic Interfaces

In addition to generic classes and methods, you can also have generic interfaces. Generic interfaces are specified just like generic classes. Here is an example. It creates an interface called **MinMax** that declares the methods **min( )** and **max( )**, which are expected to return the minimum and maximum value of some set of objects.

```
// A generic interface example.

// A Min/Max interface.
interface MinMax<T extends Comparable<T>> {
  T min();
  T max();
}

// Now, implement MinMax
class MyClass<T extends Comparable<T>> implements MinMax<T> {
  T[] vals;

  MyClass(T[] o) { vals = o; }
```

```
  // Return the minimum value in vals.
  public T min() {
    T v = vals[0];

    for(int i=1; i < vals.length; i++)
      if(vals[i].compareTo(v) < 0) v = vals[i];

    return v;
  }

  // Return the maximum value in vals.
  public T max() {
    T v = vals[0];

    for(int i=1; i < vals.length; i++)
      if(vals[i].compareTo(v) > 0) v = vals[i];

    return v;
  }
}

class GenIFDemo {
  public static void main(String args[]) {
    Integer inums[] = {3, 6, 2, 8, 6 };
    Character chs[] = {'b', 'r', 'p', 'w' };

    MyClass<Integer> iob = new MyClass<Integer>(inums);
    MyClass<Character> cob = new MyClass<Character>(chs);

    System.out.println("Max value in inums: " + iob.max());
    System.out.println("Min value in inums: " + iob.min());

    System.out.println("Max value in chs: " + cob.max());
    System.out.println("Min value in chs: " + cob.min());
  }
}
```

The output is shown here:

```
Max value in inums: 8
Min value in inums: 2
Max value in chs: w
Min value in chs: b
```

Although most aspects of this program should be easy to understand, a couple of key points need to be made. First, notice that **MinMax** is declared like this:

```
interface MinMax<T extends Comparable<T>> {
```

In general, a generic interface is declared in the same way as is a generic class. In this case, the type parameter is **T**, and it must extend **Comparable**. Notice that **Comparable** is now also generic. It takes a type parameter that specifies the type of the objects being compared.

Next, **MinMax** is implemented by **MyClass**. Notice the declaration of **MyClass**, shown here:

```
class MyClass<T extends Comparable<T>> implements MinMax<T> {
```

Pay special attention to the way that the type parameter **T** is declared by **MyClass** and then passed to **MinMax**. Because **MinMax** requires a type that extends **Comparable**, the implementing class (**MyClass** in this case) must specify the same bound. Furthermore, once this bound has been established, there is no need to specify it again in the **implements** clause. In fact, it would be wrong to do so. For example, this line is incorrect and won't compile:

```
// This is wrong!
class MyClass<T extends Comparable<T>>
        implements MinMax<T extends Comparable<T>> {
```

Once the type parameter has been established, it is simply passed to the interface without further modification.

In general, if a class implements a generic interface, then that class must also be generic, at least to the extent that it takes a type parameter that is passed to the interface. For example, the following attempt to declare **MyClass** is in error:

```
class MyClass implements MinMax<T> { // Wrong!
```

Because **MyClass** does not declare a type parameter, there is no way to pass one to **MinMax**. In this case, the identifier **T** is simply unknown and the compiler reports an error. Of course, if a class implements a *specific type* of generic interface, such as

```
class MyClass implements MinMax<Integer> { // OK
```

then the implementing class does not need to be generic.

The generic interface offers two benefits. First, it can be implemented for different types of data. Second, it allows you to put constraints (i.e., bounds) on the types of data for which the interface can be implemented. In the **MinMax** example, only types that implement the **Comparable** interface can be passed to **T**.

Here is the generalized syntax for a generic interface:

interface *interface-name<type-param-list>* { // ...

Here, *type-param-list* is a comma-separated list of type parameters. When a generic interface is implemented, you must specify the type arguments, as shown here:

class *class-name<type-param-list>*
        implements *interface-name<type-param-list>* {

Raw Types and Legacy Code

Because generics is a new feature, it was necessary for Java to provide some transition path from old, pre-generics code. Remember, there are millions and millions of lines of pre-5.0 legacy code that must remain both functional and compatible with generics. Pre-generics code must be able to work with generics, and generic code must be able to work with pre-generic code.

To handle the transition to generics, Java allows a generic class to be used without any type arguments. This creates a *raw type* for the class. This raw type is compatible with legacy code, which has no knowledge of generics. The main drawback to using the raw type is that the type safety of generics is lost.

Here is an example that shows a raw type in action:

```
// Demonstrate a raw type.
class Gen<T> {
  T ob; // declare an object of type T

  // Pass the constructor a reference to
  // an object of type T.
  Gen(T o) {
    ob = o;
  }

  // Return ob.
  T getob() {
    return ob;
```

```
    }
}

// Demonstrate raw type.
class RawDemo {
  public static void main(String args[]) {

    // Create a Gen object for Integers.
    Gen<Integer> iOb = new Gen<Integer>(88);

    // Create a Gen object for Strings.
    Gen<String> strOb = new Gen<String>("Generics Test");

    // Create a raw-type Gen object and give it
    // a Double value.
    Gen raw = new Gen(new Double(98.6));

    // Cast here is necessary because type is unknown.
    double d = (Double) raw.getob();
    System.out.println("value: " + d);

    // The use of a raw type can lead to runtime.
    // exceptions.  Here are some examples.

    // The following cast causes a runtime error!
//    int i = (Integer) raw.getob(); // runtime error

    // This assignment overrides type safety.
    strOb = raw; // OK, but potentially wrong
//    String str = strOb.getob(); // runtime error

    // This assignment also overrides type safety.
    raw = iOb; // OK, but potentially wrong
//    d = (Double) raw.getob(); // runtime error
  }
}
```

This program contains several interesting things. First, a raw type of the generic **Gen** class is created by the following declaration:

```
Gen raw = new Gen(new Double(98.6));
```

Notice that no type arguments are specified. In essence, this creates a **Gen** object whose type **T** is replaced by **Object**.

A raw type is not type-safe. Thus, a variable of a raw type can be assigned a reference to any type of **Gen** object. The reverse is also allowed; a variable of a specific **Gen** type can be assigned a reference to a raw **Gen** object. However, both operations are potentially unsafe because the type-checking mechanism of generics is circumvented.

This lack of type safety is illustrated by the commented-out lines at the end of the program. Let's examine each case. First, consider the following situation:

```
//    int i = (Integer) raw.getob(); // runtime error
```

In this statement, the value of **ob** inside **raw** is obtained and this value is cast to **Integer**. The trouble is that **raw** contains a **Double** value, not an integer value. However, this cannot be detected at compile time because the type of **raw** is unknown. Thus, this statement fails at run time.

The next sequence assigns to a **strOb** (a reference of type **Gen<String>**) a reference to a raw **Gen** object:

```
strOb = raw; // OK, but potentially wrong
//    String str = strOb.getob(); // runtime error
```

The assignment, itself, is syntactically correct, but questionable. Because **strOb** is of type **Gen<String>**, it is assumed to contain a **String**. However, after the assignment, the object referred to by **strOb** contains a **Double**. Thus, at run time, when an attempt is made to assign the contents of **strOb** to **str**, a run-time error results because **strOb** now contains a **Double**. Thus, the assignment of a raw reference to a generic reference bypasses the type-safety mechanism.

The following sequence inverts the preceding case:

```
    raw = iOb; // OK, but potentially wrong
//    d = (Double) raw.getob(); // runtime error
```

Here, a generic reference is assigned to a raw reference variable. Although this is syntactically correct, it can lead to problems, as illustrated by the second line. In this case, **raw** now refers to an object that contains an **Integer** object, but the cast assumes that it contains a **Double**. This error cannot be prevented at compile time. Rather, it causes a run-time error.

Because of the potential for danger inherent in raw types, **javac** displays *unchecked warnings* when a raw type is used in a way that might jeopardize type safety. In the preceding program, these lines generate unchecked warnings:

```
Gen raw = new Gen(new Double(98.6));

strOb = raw; // OK, but potentially wrong
```

In the first line, it is the call to the **Gen** constructor without a type argument that causes the warning. In the second line, it is the assignment of a raw reference to a generic variable that generates the warning.

At first, you might think that this line should also generate an unchecked warning, but it does not:

```
raw = iOb; // OK, but potentially wrong
```

No compiler warning is issued because the assignment does not cause any *further* loss of type safety than had already occurred when **raw** was created.

One final point: you should limit the use of raw types to those cases in which you must mix legacy code with newer, generic code. Raw types are simply a transitional feature and not something that should be used for new code.

Generic Class Hierarchies

Generic classes can be part of a class hierarchy in just the same way as a nongeneric class. Thus, a generic class can act as a superclass or be a subclass. The key difference between generic and nongeneric hierarchies is that in a generic hierarchy, any type arguments needed by a generic superclass must be passed up the hierarchy by all subclasses. This is similar to the way that constructor arguments must be passed up a hierarchy.

Using a Generic Superclass

Here is a simple example of a hierarchy that uses a generic superclass:

```
// A simple generic class hierarchy.
class Gen<T> {
  T ob;
```

```
  Gen(T o) {
    ob = o;
  }

  // Return ob.
  T getob() {
    return ob;
  }
}

// A subclass of Gen.
class Gen2<T> extends Gen<T> {
  Gen2(T o) {
    super(o);
  }
}
```

In this hierarchy, **Gen2** extends the generic class **Gen**. Notice how **Gen2** is declared by the following line:

```
class Gen2<T> extends Gen<T> {
```

The type parameter **T** is specified by **Gen2** and is also passed to **Gen** in the **extends** clause. This means that whatever type is passed to **Gen2** will also be passed to **Gen**. For example, this declaration

```
Gen2<Integer> num = new Gen2<Integer>(100);
```

passes **Integer** as the type parameter to **Gen**. Thus, the **ob** inside the **Gen** portion of **Gen2** will be of type **Integer**.

Notice also that **Gen2** does not use the type parameter **T** except to pass it to the **Gen** superclass. Thus, even if a subclass of a generic superclass would otherwise not need to be generic, it still must specify the type parameter(s) required by its generic superclass.

Of course, a subclass is free to add its own type parameters, if needed. For example, here is a variation on the preceding hierarchy in which **Gen2** adds a type parameter of its own:

```
// A subclass can add its own type parameters.
class Gen<T> {
  T ob; // declare an object of type T
```

```java
    // Pass the constructor a reference to
    // an object of type T.
    Gen(T o) {
      ob = o;.
    }

    // Return ob.
    T getob() {
      return ob;
    }
}

// A subclass of Gen that defines a second
// type parameter, called V.
class Gen2<T, V> extends Gen<T> {
  V ob2;

  Gen2(T o, V o2) {
    super(o);
    ob2 = o2;
  }

  V getob2() {
    return ob2;
  }
}

// Create an object of type Gen2.
class HierDemo {
  public static void main(String args[]) {

    // Create a Gen2 object for String and Integer.
    Gen2<String, Integer> x =
      new Gen2<String, Integer>("Value is: ", 99);

    System.out.print(x.getob());
    System.out.println(x.getob2());
  }
}
```

Notice the declaration of this version of **Gen2**, which is shown here:

```java
class Gen2<T, V> extends Gen<T> {
```

Here, **T** is the type passed to **Gen**, and **V** is the type that is specific to **Gen2**. **V** is used to declare an object called **ob2**, and as a return type for the method **getob2( )**. In **main( )**, a **Gen2** object is created in which type parameter **T** is **String**, and type parameter **V** is **Integer**. The program displays the following, expected, result:

```
Value is: 99
```

A Generic Subclass

It is perfectly acceptable for a nongeneric class to be the superclass of a generic subclass. For example, consider this program:

```
// A nongeneric class can be the superclass
// of a generic subclass.

// A nongeneric class.
class NonGen {
  int num;

  NonGen(int i) {
    num = i;
  }

  int getnum() {
    return num;
  }
}

// A generic subclass.
class Gen<T> extends NonGen {
  T ob; // declare an object of type T

  // Pass the constructor a reference to
  // an object of type T.
  Gen(T o, int i) {
    super(i);
    ob = o;
  }

  // Return ob.
  T getob() {
```

```
      return ob;
    }
  }

// Create a Gen object.
class HierDemo2 {
  public static void main(String args[]) {

    // Create a Gen object for String.
    Gen<String> w = new Gen<String>("Hello", 47);

    System.out.print(w.getob() + " ");
    System.out.println(w.getnum());
  }
}
```

The output from the program is shown here:

```
Hello 47
```

In the program, notice how **Gen** inherits **NonGen** in the following declaration:

```
class Gen<T> extends NonGen {
```

Because **NonGen** is not generic, no type argument is specified. Thus, even though **Gen** declares the type parameter **T**, it is not needed by (nor can it be used by) **NonGen**. Thus, **NonGen** is inherited by **Gen** in the normal way. No special conditions apply.

Run-Time Type Comparisons Within a Generic Hierarchy

Recall the run-time type information operator **instanceof**. It determines if an object is an instance of a class. It returns true if an object is of the specified type, or can be cast to the specified type. The **instanceof** operator can be applied to objects of generic classes. The following class demonstrates some of the type compatibility implications of a generic hierarchy:

```
// Use the instanceof operator with a generic class hierarchy.
class Gen<T> {
  T ob;
```

```
  Gen(T o) {
    ob = o;
  }

  // Return ob.
  T getob() {
    return ob;
  }
}

// A subclass of Gen.
class Gen2<T> extends Gen<T> {
  Gen2(T o) {
    super(o);
  }
}

// Demonstrate runtime type ID implications of generic class hierarchy.
class HierDemo3 {
  public static void main(String args[]) {

    // Create a Gen object for Integers.
    Gen<Integer> iOb = new Gen<Integer>(88);

    // Create a Gen2 object for Integers.
    Gen2<Integer> iOb2 = new Gen2<Integer>(99);

    // Create a Gen2 object for Strings.
    Gen2<String> strOb2 = new Gen2<String>("Generics Test");

    // See if iOb2 is some form of Gen2.
    if(iOb2 instanceof Gen2<?>)
      System.out.println("iOb2 is instance of Gen2");

    // See if iOb2 is some form of Gen.
    if(iOb2 instanceof Gen<?>)
      System.out.println("iOb2 is instance of Gen");

    System.out.println();

    // See if strOb2 is a Gen2.
    if(strOb2 instanceof Gen2<?>)
      System.out.println("strOb is instance of Gen2");
```

```
      // See if strOb2 is a Gen.
      if(strOb2 instanceof Gen<?>)
        System.out.println("strOb is instance of Gen");

      System.out.println();

      // See if iOb is an instance of Gen2, which it is not.
      if(iOb instanceof Gen2<?>)
        System.out.println("iOb is instance of Gen2");

      // See if iOb is an instance of Gen, which it is.
      if(iOb instanceof Gen<?>)
        System.out.println("iOb is instance of Gen");

      // The following can't be compiled because
      // generic type info does not exist at runtime.
//     if(iOb2 instanceof Gen2<Integer>)
//        System.out.println("iOb2 is instance of Gen2<Integer>");
    }
}
```

The output from the program is shown here:

```
iOb2 is instance of Gen2
iOb2 is instance of Gen

strOb is instance of Gen2
strOb is instance of Gen

iOb is instance of Gen
```

In this program, **Gen2** is a subclass of **Gen**, which is generic on type parameter **T**. In **main( )**, three objects are created. The first is **iOb**, which is an object of type **Gen<Integer>**. The second is **iOb2**, which is an instance of **Gen2<Integer>**. Finally, **strOb** is an object of type **Gen2<String>**.

Then, the program performs these **instanceof** tests on the type of **iOb2**:

```
// See if iOb2 is some form of Gen2.
if(iOb2 instanceof Gen2<?>)
  System.out.println("iOb2 is instance of Gen2");

// See if iOb2 is some form of Gen.
if(iOb2 instanceof Gen<?>)
  System.out.println("iOb2 is instance of Gen");
```

As the output shows, both succeed. In the first test, **iOb2** is checked against **Gen2<?>**. This test succeeds because it simply confirms that **iOb2** is an object of some type of **Gen2** object. The use of the wildcard enables **instanceof** to determine if **iOb2** is an object of any type of **Gen2**. Next, **iOb2** is tested against **Gen<?>**, the superclass type. This is also true because **iOb2** is some form of **Gen**, the superclass. The next few lines in **main( )** show the same sequence (and same results) for **strOb**.

Next, **iOb**, which is an instance of **Gen<Integer>** (the superclass), is tested by these lines:

```
// See if iOb is an instance of Gen2, which it is not.
if(iOb instanceof Gen2<?>)
  System.out.println("iOb is instance of Gen2");

// See if iOb is an instance of Gen, which it is.
if(iOb instanceof Gen<?>)
  System.out.println("iOb is instance of Gen");
```

The first **if** fails because **iOb** is not some type of **Gen2** object. The second test succeeds because **iOb** is some type of **Gen** object.

Now, look closely at these commented-out lines:

```
    // The following can't be compiled because
    // generic type info does not exist at runtime.
//    if(iOb2 instanceof Gen2<Integer>)
//       System.out.println("iOb2 is instance of Gen2<String>");
```

As the comments indicate, these lines can't be compiled because they attempt to compare **iOb2** with a specific type of **Gen2**, in this case **Gen2<Integer>**. Remember, there is no generic type information available at run time. Therefore, there is no way for **instanceof** to know if **iOb2** is an instance of **Gen2<String>** or not.

Casting

You can cast one instance of a generic class into another only if the two are otherwise compatible and their type arguments are the same. For example, assuming the foregoing program, this cast

```
(Gen<Integer>) iOb2 // legal
```

is legal because **iOb2** is an instance of **Gen<Integer>**. But, this cast

```
(Gen<Long>) iOb2 // illegal
```

is not legal because **iOb2** is not an instance of **Gen<Long>**.

Overriding Methods in a Generic Class

A method in a generic class can be overridden just like any other method. For example, consider this program in which the method **getob( )** is overridden:

```
// Overriding a generic method in a generic class.
class Gen<T> {
  T ob; // declare an object of type T

  // Pass the constructor a reference to
  // an object of type T.
  Gen(T o) {
    ob = o;
  }

  // Return ob.
  T getob() {
    System.out.print("Gen's getob(): " );
    return ob;
  }
}

// A subclass of Gen that overrides getob().
class Gen2<T> extends Gen<T> {

  Gen2(T o) {
    super(o);
  }

  // Override getob().
  T getob() {
    System.out.print("Gen2's getob(): ");
    return ob;
  }
}
```

```
// Demonstrate generic method override.
class OverrideDemo {
  public static void main(String args[]) {

    // Create a Gen object for Integers.
    Gen<Integer> iOb = new Gen<Integer>(88);

    // Create a Gen2 object for Integers.
    Gen2<Integer> iOb2 = new Gen2<Integer>(99);

    // Create a Gen2 object for Strings.
    Gen2<String> strOb2 = new Gen2<String>("Generics Test");

    System.out.println(iOb.getob());
    System.out.println(iOb2.getob());
    System.out.println(strOb2.getob());
  }
}
```

The output is shown here:

```
Gen's getob(): 88
Gen2's getob(): 99
Gen2's getob(): Generics Test
```

As the output confirms, the overridden version of **getob( )** is called for objects of type **Gen2**, but the superclass version is called for objects of type **Gen**.

Generics and Collections

As mentioned at the start of this chapter, one of the most important uses of generics is found in the Collections Framework. The Collections Framework offers classes that implement various data structures, such as lists, stacks, and queues. With the advent of Java 2, v5.0, the entire Collections Framework has been retrofitted for generics. This includes all collection classes, such as **ArrayList**, **LinkedList**, and **TreeSet**. It also means that related classes and interfaces, such as **Iterator**, are also generic. In general, the generic type parameter specifies the type of object that the collection holds and that the iterator obtains.

The use of generics fundamentally improves the type safety of the Collections Framework. To understand why, let's begin with an example that uses pre-generics code. The following program stores a list of strings in an **ArrayList** and then displays the contents of the list:

```
// Pre-generics example that uses a collection.
import java.util.*;

class OldStyle {
  public static void main(String args[]) {
    ArrayList list = new ArrayList();

    // These lines store strings, but any type of object
    // can be stored.  In old-style code, there is no
    // convenient way to restrict the type of objects stored
    // in a collection
    list.add("one");
    list.add("two");
    list.add("three");
    list.add("four");

    Iterator itr = list.iterator();
    while(itr.hasNext()) {

      // To retrieve an element, an explicit type cast is needed
      // because the collection stores only Object.
      String str = (String) itr.next(); // explicit cast needed here.

      System.out.println(str + " is " + str.length() + " chars long.");
    }
  }
}
```

Prior to generics, a collection stored references of type **Object**. This allowed any type of reference to be stored in the collection. The preceding program uses this feature to store references to objects of type **String** in **list**, but any type of reference could have been stored.

Unfortunately, the fact that a collection stored **Object** references could easily lead to errors. First, it required that you, rather than the compiler, ensured that only objects of the proper type be stored in a specific collection. For example, in the preceding example, **list** is clearly intended to store **String**s, but there is nothing that actually prevents another type of reference from being added to the collection. For example, the compiler will find nothing wrong with this line of code:

```
list.add(new Integer(100));
```

Because **list** stores **Object** references, it can store a reference to **Integer** as well as it can store a reference to **String**. However, if you intended **list** to hold only strings, then the preceding statement would corrupt the collection. Again, the compiler has no way to know that the preceding statement is invalid.

The second problem with pre-generics collections is that when you retrieve a reference from the collection, you must manually cast that reference into the proper type. This is why the preceding program casts the reference returned by **next( )** into **String**. Prior to generics, collections simply stored **Object** references and no other type information was maintained. Thus, the cast was necessary when retrieving objects from a collection.

Aside from the inconvenience of always having to cast a retrieved reference into its proper type, this lack of type information often lead to a rather serious, but surprisingly easy-to-create, error. Because **Object** can be cast into any type of object, it was possible to cast a reference obtained from a collection into the *wrong type*. For example, if the following statement were added to the preceding example, it would still compile without error, but would generate a run-time exception when executed:

```
Integer i = (Integer) itr.next();
```

Recall that the preceding example stored only references to instances of type **String** in **list**. Thus, when this statement attempts to cast a **String** into an **Integer**, an invalid cast exception results! Because this happens at run time, this is a very serious error.

The addition of generics fundamentally improves the usability and safety of collections because it

- Ensures that only references to objects of the proper type can actually be stored in a collection. Thus, a collection will always contain references of a known type.
- Eliminates the need to cast a reference retrieved from a collection. Instead, a reference retrieved from a collection is automatically cast into the proper type. This prevents run-time errors due to invalid casts and avoids an entire category of errors.

These two improvements are made possible because each collection class has been given a type parameter that specifies the type of the collection. For example, **ArrayList** is now declared like this:

class ArrayList<E>

Here, **E** is the type of elements stored in the collection. For example, the following declares an **ArrayList** for objects of type **String**:

```
ArrayList<String> list = new ArrayList<String>();
```

Now, only references of type **String** can be added to **list**.

The **Iterator** interface has also been made generic. It is now declared as shown here:

interface Iterator<E>

Here, **E** is the type of the element being iterated. This type must agree with the type of the collection for which the iterator is obtained. Furthermore, this type compatibility is enforced at compile time.

The following program shows the modern, generic form of the preceding program:

```
// Modern, generics version.
import java.util.*;

class NewStyle {
  public static void main(String args[]) {

    // Now, list holds references of type String.
    ArrayList<String> list = new ArrayList<String>();

    list.add("one");
    list.add("two");
    list.add("three");
    list.add("four");

    // Notice that Iterator is also generic.
    Iterator<String> itr = list.iterator();

    // The following statement will now cause a compile-time error.
//    Iterator<Integer> itr = list.iterator(); // Error!
```

```
while(itr.hasNext()) {
  String str = itr.next(); // no cast needed

  // Now, the following line is a compile-time,
  // rather than runtime, error
//    Integer i = itr.next(')                    t compile

    Sys+                                          .length() + " chars long.");

}
```

N   **String**. Furthermore, as
the   eturn value of **next( )**
into

Stri

The ca

   Beca   immediately update
all of yo   se generics, and you
should u   ddition of generics to
the Collec   at should be utilized
wherever

Erasure

Usually, it is n   ls about how the
Java compiler t   ever, in the case
of generics, som   t, because it
explains why the   behavior is
sometimes a bit s   y generics
are implemented i

   An important co   ws were added to
Java was the need fo   versions of Java. Simply put:
generic code had to   pre-existing, nongeneric code. Thus, any
changes to the syntax   ue Java language, or to the JVM, had to avoid breaking
older code. The way Java implements generics while satisfying this constraint is
through the use of *erasure*.

In general, here is how erasure works. When your Java code is compiled, all generic type information is removed (erased). This means replacing type parameters with their bound type, which is **Object** if no explicit bound is specified, and then applying the appropriate casts (as determined by the type arguments) to maintain type compatibility with the types specified by the type arguments. The compiler also enforces this type compatibility. This approach to generics means that no type parameters exist at run time. They are simply a source-code mechanism.

To better understand how erasure works, consider the following two classes:

```
// Here, T is bound by Object by default.
class Gen<T> {
  T ob; // here, T will be replaced by Object

  Gen(T o) {
    ob = o;
  }

  // Return ob.
  T getob() {
    return ob;
  }
}

// Here, T is bound by String.
class GenStr<T extends String> {
  T str; // here, T will be replaced by String

  GenStr(T o) {
    str = o;
  }

  T getstr() { return str; }
}
```

After these two classes are compiled, the **T** in **Gen** will be replaced by **Object**. The **T** in **GenStr** will be replaced by **String**. You can confirm this by running **javap** on their compiled classes. The results are shown here:

```
class Gen extends java.lang.Object{
    java.lang.Object ob;
    Gen(java.lang.Object);
```

```
    java.lang.Object getob();
}

class GenStr extends java.lang.Object{
    java.lang.String str;
    GenStr(java.lang.String);
    java.lang.String getstr();
}
```

Within the code for **Gen** and **GenStr**, casts are employed to ensure proper typing. For example, this sequence

```
Gen<Integer> iOb = new Gen<Integer>(99);

int x = iOb.getob();
```

would be compiled as if it were written like this:

```
Gen iOb = new Gen(99);

int x = (Integer) iOb.getob();
```

Because of erasure, some things work a bit differently than you might think. For example, consider this short program that creates two objects of the generic **Gen** class just shown:

```
class GenTypeDemo {
  public static void main(String args[]) {
    Gen<Integer> iOb = new Gen<Integer>(99);
    Gen<Float> fOb = new Gen<Float>(102.2F);

    System.out.println(iOb.getClass().getName());
    System.out.println(fOb.getClass().getName());
  }
}
```

The output from this program is shown here:

```
Gen
Gen
```

As you can see, the types of both **iOb** and **fOb** are **Gen**, not the **Gen<Integer>** and **Gen<Float>** that you might have expected. Remember, all type parameters are erased during compilation. At run time, only raw types actually exist.

Bridge Methods

Occasionally, the compiler will need to add a *bridge method* to a class to handle situations in which the type erasure of an overriding method in a subclass does not produce the same erasure as the method in the superclass. In this case, a method is generated that uses the type erasure of the superclass, and this method calls the method that has the type erasure specified by the subclass. Of course, bridge methods only occur at the bytecode level and are not seen by you, and are not available for your use.

Although bridge methods are not something that you will normally need to be concerned with, it is still instructive to see a situation in which one is generated. Consider the following program:

```
// A situation that creates a bridge method.
class Gen<T> {
  T ob; // declare an object of type T

  // Pass the constructor a reference to
  // an object of type T.
  Gen(T o) {
    ob = o;
  }

  // Return ob.
  T getob() {
    return ob;
  }
}

// A subclass of Gen.
class Gen2 extends Gen<String> {

  Gen2(String o) {
    super(o);
  }

  // A String-specific override of getob().
  String getob() {
    System.out.print("You called String getob(): ");
```

```
      return ob;
  }
}

// Demonstrate a situation that requires a bridge method.
class BridgeDemo {
  public static void main(String args[]) {

    // Create a Gen2 object for Strings.
    Gen2 strOb2 = new Gen2("Generics Test");

    System.out.println(strOb2.getob());
  }
}
```

In the program, the subclass **Gen2** extends **Gen**, but does so using a **String**-specific version of **Gen**, as its declaration shows:

```
class Gen2 extends Gen<String> {
```

Furthermore, inside **Gen2**, **getob( )** is overridden with **String** specified as the return type:

```
// A String-specific override of getob().
String getob() {
  System.out.print("You called String getob(): ");
  return ob;
}
```

All of this is perfectly acceptable. The only trouble is that because of type erasure, the expected form of **getob( )** will be

```
Object getob() { // ...
```

To handle this problem, the compiler generates a bridge method with the preceding signature that calls the **String** version. Thus, if you examine the class file for **Gen2** by using **javap**, you will see the following methods:

```
class Gen2 extends Gen{
    Gen2(java.lang.String);
    java.lang.String getob();
    java.lang.Object getob(); // bridge method
}
```

As you can see, the bridge method has been included. (The comment was added by the author, and not by **javap**.)

There is one last point to make about bridge methods. Notice that the only difference between the two **getob( )** methods is their return type. Normally, this would cause an error, but because this does not occur in your source code, it does not cause a problem and is handled correctly by the JVM.

Ambiguity Errors

The inclusion of generics gives rise to a new type of error that you must guard against: *ambiguity*. Ambiguity errors occur when erasure causes two seemingly distinct generic declarations to resolve to the same erased type, causing a conflict. Here is an example that involves method overloading:

```
// Ambiguity caused by erasure on
// overloaded methods.
class MyGenClass<T, V> {
  T ob1;
  V ob2;

  // ...

  // These two overloaded methods are ambiguous
  // and will not compile.
  void set(T o) {
    ob1 = o;
  }

  void set(V o) {
    ob2 = o;
  }
}
```

Notice that **MyGenClass** declares two generic types: **T** and **V**. Inside **MyGenClass**, an attempt is made to overload **set( )** based on parameters of type **T** and **V**. This looks reasonable because **T** and **V** appear to be different types. However, there are two ambiguity problems here.

First (as **MyGenClass** is written) there is no requirement that **T** and **V** actually be different types. For example, it is perfectly correct (in principle) to construct a **MyGenClass** object as shown here:

```
MyGenClass<String, String> obj = new MyGenClass<String, String>()
```

In this case, both **T** and **V** will be replaced by **String**. This makes both versions of **set( )** identical, which is, of course, an error.

Second, and more fundamental, is that the type erasure of **set( )** reduces both versions to the following:

```
void set(Object o) { // ...
```

Thus, the overloading of **set( )** as attempted in **MyGenClass** is inherently ambiguous.

Ambiguity errors can be tricky to fix. For example, if you know that **V** will always be some type of **String**, you might try to fix **MyGenClass** by rewriting its declaration as shown here:

```
class MyGenClass<T, V extends String> {  // almost OK!
```

This change causes **MyGenClass** to compile, and you can even instantiate objects like the one shown here:

```
MyGenClass<Integer, String> x = new MyGenClass<Integer, String>();
```

This works because Java can accurately determine which method to call. However, ambiguity returns when you try this line:

```
MyGenClass<String, String> x = new MyGenClass<String, String>();
```

In this case, since both **T** and **V** are **String**, which version of **set( )** is to be called?

Frankly, in the preceding example, it would be much better to use two separate method names than to try to overload **set( )**. Often, the solution to ambiguity involves the restructuring of the code, because ambiguity often means that you have a conceptual error in your design.

Some Generic Restrictions

There are a few restrictions that you need to keep in mind when using generics. They involve creating objects of a type parameter, static members, exceptions, and arrays. Each is examined here.

Type Parameters Can't Be Instantiated

It is not possible to create an instance of a type parameter. For example, consider this class:

```
// Can't create an instance of T.
class Gen<T> {
  T ob;
  Gen() {
    ob = new T(); // Illegal!!!
  }
}
```

Here, it is illegal to attempt to create an instance of **T**. The reason should be easy to understand: because **T** does not exist at run time, how would the compiler know what type of object to create? Remember, erasure removes all type parameters during the compilation process.

Restrictions on static Members

No **static** member can use a type parameter declared by the enclosing class. For example, all of the **static** members of this class are illegal:

```
class Wrong<T> {
  // Wrong, no static variables of type T.
  static T ob;

  // Wrong, no static method can use T.
  static T getob() {
    return ob;
  }

  // Wrong, no static method can access object
  // of type T.
  static void showob() {
    System.out.println(ob);
  }
}
```

Although you can't declare **static** members that use a type parameter declared by the enclosing class, you *can* declare **static** generic methods, which define their own type parameters, as was done earlier in this chapter.

Generic Array Restrictions

There are two important generics restrictions that apply to arrays. First, you cannot instantiate an array whose base type is a type parameter. Second, you cannot create an array of type-specific generic references. The following short program shows both situations:

```
// Generics and arrays.
class Gen<T extends Number> {
  T ob;

  T vals[]; // OK

  Gen(T o, T[] nums) {
    ob = o;

    // This statement is illegal.
    // vals = new T[10]; // can't create an array of T

    // But, this statement is OK.
    vals = nums; // OK to assign reference to existent array
  }
}

class GenArrays {
  public static void main(String args[]) {
    Integer n[] = { 1, 2, 3, 4, 5 };

    Gen<Integer> iOb = new Gen<Integer>(50, n);

    // Can't create an array of type-specific generic references.
    // Gen<Integer> gens[] = new Gen<Integer>[10]; // Wrong!

    // This is OK.
    Gen<?> gens[] = new Gen<?>[10]; // OK
  }
}
```

As the program shows, it's valid to declare a reference to an array of type **T**, as this line does:

```
T vals[]; // OK
```

But, you cannot instantiate an array of T, as this commented-out line attempts:

```
// vals = new T[10]; // can't create an array of T
```

The reason you can't create an array of **T** is that **T** does not exist at run time, so there is no way for the compiler to know what type of array to actually create.

However, you can pass a reference to a type-compatible array to **Gen( )** when an object is created and assign that reference to **vals**, as the program does in this line:

```
vals = nums; // OK to assign reference to existent array
```

This works because the array passed to **Gen** has a known type, which will be the same type as **T** at the time of object creation.

Inside **main( )**, notice that you can't declare an array of references to a specific generic type. That is, this line

```
// Gen<Integer> gens[] = new Gen<Integer>[10]; // Wrong!
```

won't compile. Arrays of specific generic types simply aren't allowed because they can lead to a loss of type safety.

You *can* create an array of references to a generic type if you use a wildcard, however, as shown here:

```
Gen<?> gens[] = new Gen<?>[10]; // OK
```

This approach is better than using an array of raw types because at least some type checking will still be enforced.

Generic Exception Restriction

A generic class cannot extend **Throwable**. This means that you cannot create generic exception classes.

Final Thoughts on Generics

Generics are a powerful extension to Java because they streamline the creation of type-safe, reusable code. Although the generic syntax can seem a bit overwhelming at first, it will become second nature after you use it a while. Frankly, generic code will be a part of all Java programmers' future.

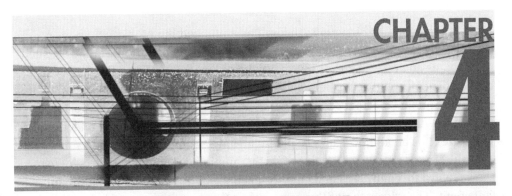

CHAPTER 4

The For-Each Version
of the for Loop

C ontemporary language theory has embraced the "for-each" loop. A for-each loop is designed to cycle through a collection of objects, such as an array, in strictly sequential fashion, from start to finish. Because of the convenience that it offers, the for-each loop is quickly becoming a feature that programmers demand. Earlier versions of Java did not support a for-each loop, but with the release of Java 2, v5.0, this feature has now been added to the language. It is an addition sure to please all Java programmers.

Unlike some languages, such as C#, that implement a for-each loop by using the keyword **foreach**, Java adds the for-each capability by enhancing the **for** statement. The advantage of this approach is that no new keyword is required, and no preexisting code is broken. The for-each style of **for** is also referred to as the *enhanced* **for** loop, and both terms are used here.

For-Each Fundamentals

The general form of the for-each version of the **for** is shown here:

for(*type itr-var* : *iterableObj*) *statement-block*

Here, *type* specifies the type and *itr-var* specifies the name of an *iteration variable* that will receive the elements contained in *iterableObj*, one at a time, from beginning to end. The object referred to by *iterableObj* must be an array or an object that implements the new **Iterable** interface. In all cases, *type* must be the same as (or compatible with) the elements retrieved from *iterableObj*. Thus, when iterating over arrays, *type* must be compatible with the base type of the array. With each iteration of the loop, the next element in *iterableObj* is retrieved and stored in *itr-var*. The loop repeats until all elements have been obtained.

To understand the motivation behind a for-each style loop, consider the type of **for** loop that it is designed to replace. The following fragment uses a traditional **for** loop to compute the sum of the values in an array:

```
int nums[] = { 1, 2, 3, 4, 5, 6, 7, 8, 9, 10 };
int sum = 0;

for(int i=0; i < 10; i++) sum += nums[i];
```

To compute the sum, each element in **nums** is read, in order, from start to finish. Thus, the entire array is read in strictly sequential order. This is accomplished by manually indexing the **nums** array by **i**, the loop control variable. Furthermore, the starting and ending value for the loop control variable, and its increment, must be explicitly specified.

The for-each style **for** automates the preceding loop. Specifically, it eliminates the need to establish a loop counter, specify a starting and ending value, and manually index the array. Instead, it automatically cycles through the entire array, obtaining one element at a time, in sequence, from beginning to end. For example, here is the preceding fragment rewritten using the for-each version of the **for**:

```
int nums[] = { 1, 2, 3, 4, 5, 6, 7, 8, 9, 10 };
int sum = 0;

for(int x: nums) sum += x;
```

With each pass through the loop, **x** is automatically given a value equal to the next element in **nums**. Thus, on the first iteration, **x** contains 1, on the second iteration, **x** contains 2, and so on. Not only is the syntax streamlined, it also prevents boundary errors.

Here is an entire program that demonstrates the for-each version of the **for** just described:

```
// Use a for-each style for loop.
class ForEach {
  public static void main(String args[]) {
    int nums[] = { 1, 2, 3, 4, 5, 6, 7, 8, 9, 10 };
    int sum = 0;

    // use for-each style for to display and sum the values
    for(int x : nums) {
      System.out.println("Value is: " + x);
      sum += x;
    }

    System.out.println("Summation: " + sum);
  }
}
```

The output from the program is shown here:

```
Value is: 1
Value is: 2
Value is: 3
Value is: 4
Value is: 5
Value is: 6
Value is: 7
Value is: 8
Value is: 9
Value is: 10
Summation: 55
```

As this output shows, the for-each style **for** automatically cycles through an array in sequence from the lowest index to the highest.

Although the for-each **for** loop iterates until all elements in an array have been examined, it is possible to terminate the loop early by using a **break** statement. For example, this program sums only the first five elements of **nums**:

```
// Use break with a for-each style for.
class ForEach2 {
  public static void main(String args[]) {
    int sum = 0;
    int nums[] = { 1, 2, 3, 4, 5, 6, 7, 8, 9, 10 };

    // Use for to display and sum the values.
    for(int x : nums) {
      System.out.println("Value is: " + x);
      sum += x;
      if(x == 5) break; // stop the loop when 5 is obtained
    }
    System.out.println("Summation of first 5 elements: " + sum);
  }
}
```

This is the output produced:

```
Value is: 1
Value is: 2
```

```
Value is: 3
Value is: 4
Value is: 5
Summation of first 5 elements: 15
```

As is evident, the **for** loop stops after the fifth element has been obtained.

There is one important point to understand about the for-each style loop. Its iteration variable is "read-only" as it relates to the underlying array. An assignment to the iteration variable has no effect on the underlying array. In other words, you can't change the contents of the array by assigning the iteration variable a new value. For example, consider this program:

```java
// The for-each loop is essentially read-only.
class NoChange {
  public static void main(String args[]) {
    int nums[] = { 1, 2, 3, 4, 5, 6, 7, 8, 9, 10 };

    for(int x : nums) {
      System.out.print(x + " ");
      x = x * 10; // no effect on nums
    }

    System.out.println();

    for(int x : nums)
      System.out.print(x + " ");

    System.out.println();
  }
}
```

The first **for** loop increases the value of the iteration variable by a factor of 10. However, this assignment has no effect on the underlying array **nums**, as the second **for** loop illustrates. The output, shown here, proves this point:

```
1 2 3 4 5 6 7 8 9 10
1 2 3 4 5 6 7 8 9 10
```

Iterating over Multidimensional Arrays

The enhanced version of the **for** also works on multidimensional arrays. Remember, however, that in Java, multidimensional arrays consist of *arrays of arrays*. (For example, a two-dimensional array is an array of one-dimensional arrays.) This is important when iterating over a multidimensional array because each iteration obtains the *next array,* not an individual element. Furthermore, the iteration variable in the **for** loop must be compatible with the type of array being obtained. For example, in the case of a two-dimensional array, the iteration variable must be a reference to a one-dimensional array. In general, when using the for-each **for** to iterate over an array of N dimensions, the objects obtained will be arrays of $N-1$ dimensions. To understand the implications of this, consider the following program. It uses nested **for** loops to obtain the elements of a two-dimensional array in row-order, from first to last.

```
// Use for-each style for on a two-dimensional array.
class ForEach3 {
  public static void main(String args[]) {
    int sum = 0;
    int nums[][] = new int[3][5];

    // give nums some values
    for(int i = 0; i < 3; i++)
      for(int j=0; j < 5; j++)
        nums[i][j] = (i+1)*(j+1);

    // use for-each for to display and sum the values
    for(int x[] : nums) {
      for(int y : x) {
        System.out.println("Value is: " + y);
        sum += y;
      }
    }
    System.out.println("Summation: " + sum);
  }
}
```

The output from this program is shown here:

```
Value is: 1
Value is: 2
```

```
Value is: 3
Value is: 4
Value is: 5
Value is: 2
Value is: 4
Value is: 6
Value is: 8
Value is: 10
Value is: 3
Value is: 6
Value is: 9
Value is: 12
Value is: 15
Summation: 90
```

In the program, pay special attention to this line:

```
for(int x[] : nums) {
```

Notice how **x** is declared. It is a reference to a one-dimensional array of integers. This is necessary because each iteration of the **for** obtains the next *array* in **nums**, beginning with the array specified by **nums[0]**. The inner **for** loop then cycles through each of these arrays, displaying the values of each element.

Applying the For-Each for

Since the for-each style **for** can only cycle through an array sequentially, from start to finish, you might think that its use is limited, but this is not true. A large number of algorithms require exactly this mechanism. One of the most common is searching. For example, the following program uses a **for** loop to search an unsorted array for a value. It stops if the value is found.

```
// Search an array using for-each style for.
class Search {
  public static void main(String args[]) {
    int nums[] = { 6, 8, 3, 7, 5, 6, 1, 4 };
    int val = 5;
    boolean found = false;

    // use for-each style for to search nums for val
```

```
    for(int x : nums) {
      if(x == val) {
        found = true;
        break;
      }
    }

    if(found)
      System.out.println("Value found!");
  }
}
```

The for-each style **for** is an excellent choice in this application because searching an unsorted array involves examining each element in sequence. (Of course, if the array were sorted, a binary search could be used, which would require a different style loop.) Other types of applications that benefit from for-each style loops include computing an average, finding the minimum or maximum of a set, looking for duplicates, and so on.

Using the For-Each Loop with Collections

Although the preceding examples have used arrays, the for-each form of the **for** loop is not limited to this use. It can be used to cycle through the elements of any object that implements the **Iterable** interface. This includes all collections defined by the Collections Framework, which have been retrofitted by Java 2, v5.0 to implement the **Iterable** interface. In the past, iterating through a collection required that you obtain an iterator and manually call its **hasNext( )** and **next( )** methods. The enhanced **for** loop now automates this process.

The following program demonstrates the use of the **for** loop to iterate through an **ArrayList** collection that contains numeric values. The program computes the average of the values in the list.

```
// Using a for-each for loop with a collection.
import java.util.*;

class AvgCollection {
  static double getAvg(ArrayList<Double> nums) {
```

```
      double sum = 0.0;

    for(double itr : nums)
      sum = sum + itr;

    return sum / nums.size();
  }

  public static void main(String args[]) {
    ArrayList<Double> list = new ArrayList<Double>();

    list.add(10.14);
    list.add(20.22);
    list.add(30.78);
    list.add(40.46);

    double avg = getAvg(list);

    System.out.println("List average is " + avg);

  }
}
```

The following output is produced:

```
List average is 25.4
```

In the **getAvg( )** method, this for-each **for** loop

```
for(double itr : nums)
  sum = sum + itr;
```

replaces the following equivalent code that uses explicit iteration:

```
Iterator<Double> itr = nums.iterator();
while(itr.hasNext()) {
  Double d = itr.next();
  sum = sum + d;
}
```

As you can see, the **for** loop is substantially shorter, and more to the point.

One other point: If you want to use the enhanced **for** to cycle through the contents of a collection given the collection's raw type, then the iteration variable must be of type **Object**. This means that the iteration variable will need to be explicitly cast to the target type. Frankly, it is best to avoid the use of raw types, whether for use in the **for** or in general. Generics offer a better, safer, more convenient alternative.

Creating Iterable Objects

Although the for-each form of the **for** loop was designed with arrays and collections in mind, it can be used to cycle through the contents of any object that implements the **Iterable** interface. This enables you to create classes whose objects can be used with the for-each form of the **for** loop. This is a powerful feature that substantially increases the types of programming situations to which the **for** can be applied.

Iterable is a generic interface that was added by Java 2, v5.0. It is defined in **java.lang** and declared like this:

    interface Iterable<T>

Here, **T** is the type of element that will be stored by the object, which is also the type of object obtained by each iteration of a **for** loop.

Iterable contains only one method, **iterator( )**, shown here:

    Iterator<T> iterator( )

This method returns an **Iterator** to the elements contained in the invoking object. Notice that **Iterator** is a generic class. Earlier versions of **Iterator** were not generic. **Iterator** was made generic by Java 2, v5.0, when the entire Collections Framework was retrofitted for generics. Here, **T** specifies the type of element that will be iterated.

Because the **iterator( )** method of **Iterable** returns an **Iterator**, often a class that implements **Iterable** will also implement **Iterator**. **Iterator** is defined like this:

    interface Iterator<E>

Here, **E** specifies the type of element being iterated. **Iterator** defines the following methods.

Method	Description
boolean hasNext( )	Returns **true** if there are more elements. Otherwise, returns **false**.
E next( )	Returns the next element. Throws **NoSuchElementException** if there is not a next element.
void remove( )	Removes the current element. This method is optional. Throws **IllegalStateException** if an attempt is made to call **remove( )** that is not preceded by a call to **next( )**. Throws **UnsupportedOperationException** if this action is not implemented.

As their descriptions suggest, an object being iterated will return true if it still has elements to supply when **hasNext( )** is called. It will return the next element when **next( )** is called. The **remove( )** method need not be implemented.

When an **Iterable** object is used in a for-each style **for** loop, implicit calls to methods defined by **Iterable** and **Iterator** are made. Therefore, instead of having to call methods such as **hasNext( )** or **next( )** manually, the **for** calls them for you, implicitly.

Here is an example that creates an **Iterable** object called **StrIterable**, which implements an **Iterator** that cycles through the characters that comprise a string. Inside **main( )**, a **StrIterable** is created and its elements are obtained one at a time through the use of a for-each style **for** loop.

```java
// Using a for-each for loop on an Iterable object.
import java.util.*;

// This class supports iteration of the
// characters that comprise a string.
class StrIterable implements Iterable<Character>,
                             Iterator<Character> {
  private String str;
  private int count = 0;

  StrIterable(String s) {
    str = s;
  }

  // The next three methods implement Iterator.
  public boolean hasNext() {
```

```
      if(count < str.length()) return true;
      return false;
    }

  public Character next() {
    if(count == str.length())
      throw new NoSuchElementException();

    count++;
    return str.charAt(count-1);
  }

  public void remove() {
    throw new UnsupportedOperationException();
  }

  // This method implements Iterable.
  public Iterator<Character> iterator() {
    return this;
  }
}

class ForEachIterable {
  public static void main(String args[]) {
    StrIterable x = new StrIterable("This is a test.");

    // Show each character.
    for(char ch : x)
      System.out.print(ch);

    System.out.println();
  }
}
```

The output is shown here:

```
This is a test.
```

In **main( )**, a **StrIterable** called **x** is constructed and passed the string "This is a test." This string is stored in the **str** member of **StrIterable**. Next, a for-each style **for** loop is set up to cycle through the contents of **x**. Each pass through the loop obtains the next character in the string. This is accomplished behind the scenes with implicit calls to the **Iterable** and **Iterator** methods. You can use the preceding code as a model for any type of object that you want to be able to iterate over using an enhanced **for** loop.

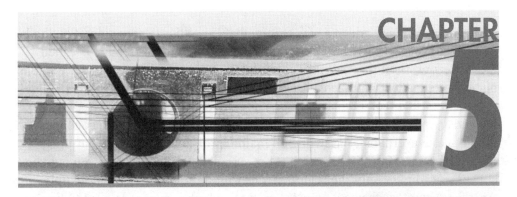

CHAPTER
5

Varargs:
Variable-Length
Arguments

J ava 2, v5.0 has added a new feature that simplifies the creation of methods that need to take a variable number of arguments. This feature is called *varargs,* short for *variable-length arguments.* A method that takes a variable number of arguments is called a *variable-arity method,* or simply a *varargs method.*

Situations that require that a variable number of arguments be passed to a method are not unusual. For example, a method that opens an Internet connection might take a username, password, filename, protocol, and so on, but provide defaults if some of this information is not supplied. In this situation, it would be convenient to pass only the arguments to which the defaults did not apply. Another example is the new **printf( )** method, which is part of Java's I/O library. As you will see in Chapter 9, it takes a variable number of arguments, which it formats and then outputs.

Varargs Fundamentals

Prior to Java 2, v5.0, variable-length arguments could be handled in either of two ways, neither of which was particularly pleasing. First, if the maximum number of arguments was small and known, then you could create overloaded versions of the method, one for each way the method could be called. Although this works and is suitable for some situations, it applies to only a narrow class of situations.

In cases where the maximum number of potential arguments was larger, or unknowable, a second approach was used in which the arguments were put into an array, and then the array was passed to the method. This approach is illustrated by the following program:

```
// Use an array to pass a variable number of
// arguments to a method. This is the old-style
// approach to variable-length arguments.
class PassArray {
  static void vaTest(int v[]) {
    System.out.print("Number of args: " + v.length +
                     " Contents: ");

    for(int x : v)
      System.out.print(x + " ");

    System.out.println();
```

```
  }

  public static void main(String args[])
  {
    // Notice how an array must be created to
    // hold the arguments.
    int n1[] = { 10 };
    int n2[] = { 1, 2, 3 };
    int n3[] = { };

    vaTest(n1); // 1 arg
    vaTest(n2); // 3 args
    vaTest(n3); // no args
  }
}
```

The output from the program is shown here:

```
Number of args: 1 Contents: 10
Number of args: 3 Contents: 1 2 3
Number of args: 0 Contents:
```

In the program, the method **vaTest( )** is passed its arguments through the array **v**. This old-style approach to variable-length arguments does enable **vaTest( )** to take an arbitrary number of arguments. However, it requires that these arguments be manually packaged into an array prior to calling **vaTest( )**. Not only is it tedious to construct an array each time **vaTest( )** is called, it is potentially error-prone. The new varargs feature offers a simpler, better option.

A variable-length argument is specified by three periods (**...**). For example, here is how **vaTest( )** is written using a vararg:

```
static void vaTest(int ... v) {
```

This syntax tells the compiler that **vaTest( )** can be called with zero or more arguments. As a result, **v** is implicitly declared as an array of type **int[ ]**. Thus, inside **vaTest( )**, **v** is accessed using the normal array syntax. Here is the preceding program rewritten using a vararg:

```
// Demonstrate variable-length arguments.
class VarArgs {
```

```
    // vaTest() now uses a vararg.
    static void vaTest(int ... v) {
      System.out.print("Number of args: " + v.length +
                          " Contents: ");

      for(int x : v)
        System.out.print(x + " ");

      System.out.println();
    }

    public static void main(String args[])
    {

      // Notice how vaTest() can be called with a
      // variable number of arguments.
      vaTest(10);        // 1 arg
      vaTest(1, 2, 3); // 3 args
      vaTest();          // no args
    }
}
```

The output from the program is the same as the original version.

There are two important things to notice about this program. First, as explained, inside **vaTest( )**, **v** is operated on as an array. This is because **v** *is* an array. The **...** syntax simply tells the compiler that a variable number of arguments will be used, and that these arguments will be stored in the array referred to by **v**. Second, in **main( )**, **vaTest( )** is called with different numbers of arguments, including no arguments at all. The arguments are automatically put in an array and passed to **v**. In the case of no arguments, the length of the array is zero.

A method can have "normal" parameters along with a variable-length parameter. However, the variable-length parameter must be the last parameter declared by the method. For example, this method declaration is perfectly acceptable:

```
int doIt(int a, int b, double c, int ... vals) {
```

In this case, the first three arguments used in a call to **doIt( )** are matched to the first three parameters. Then, any remaining arguments are assumed to belong to **vals**.

Remember, the varargs parameter must be last. For example, the following declaration is incorrect:

```
int doIt(int a, int b, double c, int ... vals, boolean stopFlag) { // Error!
```

Here, there is an attempt to declare a regular parameter after the varargs parameter, which is illegal.

There is one more restriction to be aware of: there must be only one varargs parameter. For example, this declaration is also invalid:

```
int doIt(int a, int b, double c, int ... vals, double ... morevals) { // Error!
```

The attempt to declare the second varargs parameter is illegal.

Here is a reworked version of the **vaTest( )** method that takes a regular argument and a variable-length argument:

```
// Use varargs with standard arguments.
class VarArgs2 {

  // Here, msg is a normal parameter and v is a
  // varargs parameter.
  static void vaTest(String msg, int ... v) {
    System.out.print(msg + v.length +
                        " Contents: ");

    for(int x : v)
      System.out.print(x + " ");

    System.out.println();
  }

  public static void main(String args[])
  {
    vaTest("One vararg: ", 10);
    vaTest("Three varargs: ", 1, 2, 3);
    vaTest("No varargs: ");
  }
}
```

The output from this program is shown here:

```
One vararg: 1 Contents: 10
Three varargs: 3 Contents: 1 2 3
No varargs: 0 Contents:
```

Overloading Vararg Methods

You can overload a method that takes a variable-length argument. For example, the following program overloads **vaTest( )** three times:

```java
// Varargs and overloading.
class VarArgs3 {

  static void vaTest(int ... v) {
    System.out.print("vaTest(int ...): " +
                     "Number of args: " + v.length +
                     " Contents: ");

    for(int x : v)
      System.out.print(x + " ");

    System.out.println();
  }

  static void vaTest(boolean ... v) {
    System.out.print("vaTest(boolean ...) " +
                     "Number of args: " + v.length +
                     " Contents: ");

    for(boolean x : v)
      System.out.print(x + " ");

    System.out.println();
  }

  static void vaTest(String msg, int ... v) {
    System.out.print("vaTest(String, int ...): " +
                     msg + v.length +
                     " Contents: ");
```

```
    for(int x : v)
      System.out.print(x + " ");

    System.out.println();
  }

  public static void main(String args[])
  {
    vaTest(1, 2, 3);
    vaTest("Testing: ", 10, 20);
    vaTest(true, false, false);
  }
}
```

The output produced by this program is shown here:

```
vaTest(int ...): Number of args: 3 Contents: 1 2 3
vaTest(String, int ...): Testing: 2 Contents: 10 20
vaTest(boolean ...) Number of args: 3 Contents: true false false
```

This program illustrates both ways that a varargs method can be overloaded. First, the types of its vararg parameter can differ. This is the case for **vaTest(int ...)** and **vaTest(boolean ...)**. Remember, the **...** causes the parameter to be treated as an array of the specified type. Therefore, just as you can overload methods by using different types of array parameters, you can overload varargs methods by using different types of varargs. In this case, Java uses the type difference to determine which overloaded method to call.

The second way to overload a varargs method is to add a normal parameter. This is what was done with **vaTest(String, int ...)**. In this case, Java uses both the number of arguments and the type of the arguments to determine which method to call.

Varargs and Ambiguity

Somewhat unexpected errors can result when overloading a method that takes a variable-length argument. These errors involve ambiguity because it is possible to create an ambiguous call to an overloaded varargs method. For example, consider the following program:

```
// Varargs, overloading, and ambiguity.
//
// This program contains an error and will
// not compile!
class VarArgs4 {

  static void vaTest(int ... v) {
    System.out.print("vaTest(int ...): " +
                     "Number of args: " + v.length +
                     " Contents: ");

    for(int x : v)
      System.out.print(x + " ");

    System.out.println();
  }

  static void vaTest(boolean ... v) {
    System.out.print("vaTest(boolean ...) " +
                     "Number of args: " + v.length +
                     " Contents: ");

    for(boolean x : v)
      System.out.print(x + " ");

    System.out.println();
  }


  public static void main(String args[])
  {
    vaTest(1, 2, 3);  // OK
    vaTest(true, false, false); // OK

    vaTest(); // Error: Ambiguous!
  }
}
```

In this program, the overloading of **vaTest( )** is perfectly correct. However, this program will not compile because of the following call:

```
vaTest(); // Error: Ambiguous!
```

Because the vararg parameter can be empty, this call could be translated into a call to **vaTest(int ...)** or **vaTest(boolean ...)**. Both are equally valid. Thus, the call is inherently ambiguous.

Here is another example of ambiguity. The following overloaded versions of **vaTest( )** are inherently ambiguous even though one takes a normal parameter:

```
static void vaTest(int ... v) { // ...
```

```
static void vaTest(int n, int ... v) { // ...
```

Although the parameter lists of **vaTest( )** differ, there is no way for the compiler to resolve the following call:

    vaTest(1)

Does this translate into a call to **vaTest(int ...)**, with one vararg argument, or into a call to **vaTest(int, int ...)**, with no varargs arguments? There is no way for the compiler to answer this question. Thus, the situation is ambiguous.

Because of ambiguity errors like those just shown, sometimes you will need to forego overloading and simply use two different method names. Also, in some cases, ambiguity errors expose a conceptual flaw in your code, which you can remedy by more carefully crafting a solution.

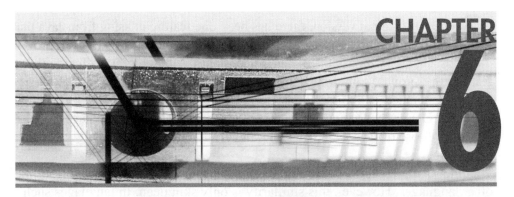

Enumerations

ince its original version, there has been one feature missing from Java that many programmers felt was needed: enumerations. In its simplest form, an *enumeration* is a list of named constants. Although Java offered other features that provide somewhat similar functionality, such as **final** variables, many programmers still missed the conceptual purity of enumerations—especially because enumerations are supported by most other commonly used languages. With the release of Java 2, v5.0, enumerations are now available to the Java programmer.

In their simplest form, Java enumerations appear similar to enumerations in other languages. However, this similarity is only skin deep. In languages such as C++, enumerations are simply lists of named integer constants. In Java, an enumeration defines a class type. By making enumerations into classes, the concept of the enumeration is greatly expanded. For example, in Java, an enumeration can have constructors, methods, and instance variables. Therefore, although enumerations were several years in the making, Java's implementation has made them well worth the wait.

Enumeration Fundamentals

An enumeration is created using the new **enum** keyword. For example, here is a simple enumeration that lists various apple varieties:

```
// An enumeration of apple varieties.
enum Apple {
  Jonathan, GoldenDel, RedDel, Winesap, Cortland
}
```

The identifiers **Jonathan, GoldenDel**, and so on, are called *enumeration constants*. Each is implicitly declared as a public, static member of **Apple**. Furthermore, their type is the type of the enumeration in which they are declared, which is **Apple** in this case. Thus, in the language of Java, these constants are called *self-typed,* in which "self" refers to the enclosing enumeration.

Once you have defined an enumeration, you can create a variable of that type. However, even though enumerations define a class type, you do not instantiate an **enum** using **new**. Instead, you declare and use an enumeration variable in much the same way as you do one of the primitive types, such as **int** or **char**. For example, this declares **ap** as a variable of enumeration type **Apple**:

```
Apple ap;
```

Because **ap** is of type **Apple**, the only values that it can be assigned (or contain) are those defined by the enumeration. For example, this assigns **ap** the value **RedDel**:

```
ap = Apple.RedDel;
```

Notice that the symbol **RedDel** is preceded by **Apple**.

Two enumeration constants can be compared for equality by using the = = relational operator. For example, this statement compares the value in **ap** with the **GoldenDel** constant:

```
if(ap == Apple.GoldenDel) // ...
```

An enumeration value can also be used to control a **switch** statement. Of course, all of the **case** statements must use constants from the same **enum** as that used by the **switch** expression. For example, this **switch** is perfectly valid:

```
// Use an enum to control a switch statement.
switch(ap) {
  case Jonathan:
    // ...
  case Winesap:
    // ...
```

Notice that in the **case** statements, the names of the enumeration constants are used without being qualified by their enumeration type name. That is, **Winesap**, not **Apple.Winesap**, is used. This is because the type of the enumeration in the **switch** expression has already implicitly specified the **enum** type of the **case** constants. There is no need to qualify the constants in the **case** statements with their **enum** type name.

When an enumeration constant is displayed, such as in a **println( )** statement, its name is output. For example, given the statement

```
System.out.println(Apple.Winesap);
```

the name **Winesap** is displayed.

The following program puts together all of the pieces and demonstrates the **Apple** enumeration:

```java
// An enumeration of apple varieties.
enum Apple {
  Jonathan, GoldenDel, RedDel, Winesap, Cortland
}

class EnumDemo {
  public static void main(String args[])
  {
    Apple ap;

    ap = Apple.RedDel;

    // Output an enum value.
    System.out.println("Value of ap: " + ap);
    System.out.println();

    ap = Apple.GoldenDel;

    // Compare two enum values.
    if(ap == Apple.GoldenDel)
      System.out.println("ap contains GoldenDel.\n");

    // Use an enum to control a switch statement.
    switch(ap) {
      case Jonathan:
        System.out.println("Jonathan is red.");
        break;
      case GoldenDel:
        System.out.println("Golden Delicious is yellow.");
        break;
      case RedDel:
        System.out.println("Red Delicious is red.");
        break;
      case Winesap:
        System.out.println("Winesap is red.");
        break;
```

```
      case Cortland:
        System.out.println("Cortland is red.");
        break;
    }
  }
}
```

The output from the program is shown here:

```
Value of ap: RedDel

ap contains GoldenDel.

Golden Delicious is yellow.
```

The values( ) and valueOf( ) Methods

All enumerations automatically contain two predefined methods: **values( )** and **valueOf( )**. Their general forms are shown here:

> public static *enum-type*[ ] values( )

> public static *enum-type* valueOf(String *str*)

The **values( )** method returns an array that contains a list of the enumeration constants. The **valueOf( )** method returns the enumeration constant whose value corresponds to the string passed in *str*. In both cases, *enum-type* is the type of the enumeration. For example, in the case of the **Apple** enumeration shown earlier, the return type of **valueOf( )** is **Apple**.

The following program demonstrates the **values( )** and **valueOf( )** methods:

```
// Use the built-in enumeration methods.

// An enumeration of apple varieties.
enum Apple {
  Jonathan, GoldenDel, RedDel, Winesap, Cortland
}
```

```
class EnumDemo2 {
  public static void main(String args[])
  {
    Apple ap;

    System.out.println("Here are all Apple constants");

    // use values()
    Apple allapples[] = Apple.values();
    for(Apple a : allapples)
      System.out.println(a);

    System.out.println();

    // use valueOf()
    ap = Apple.valueOf("Winesap");
    System.out.println("ap contains " + ap);

  }
}
```

The output from the program is shown here:

```
Here are all Apple constants
Jonathan
GoldenDel
RedDel
Winesap
Cortland


ap contains Winesap
```

Notice that this program uses a for-each style **for** loop to cycle through the array of constants obtained by calling **values( )**. For the sake of illustration, the variable **allapples** was created and assigned a reference to the enumeration array. However, this step is not necessary because the **for** could have been written as shown here, eliminating the need for the **allapples** variable:

```
for(Apple a : Apple.values())
  System.out.println(a);
```

Now, notice how the value corresponding to the name **Winesap** was obtained by calling **valueOf( )**:

```
ap = Apple.valueOf("Winesap");
```

As explained, **valueOf( )** returns the enumeration value associated with the name of the constant represented as a string.

> **NOTE**
>
> *C/C++ programmers will notice that Java makes it much easier to translate between the human-readable form of an enumeration constant and its binary value than do these other languages. This is a significant advantage to Java's approach to enumerations.*

Java Enumerations Are Class Types

As explained, a Java enumeration is a class type. Although you don't instantiate an **enum** using **new**, enumerations otherwise have much the same capabilities as other classes. The fact that **enum** defines a class gives the Java enumeration powers that enumerations in other languages simply do not have. For example, you can give them constructors, add instance variables and methods, and even implement interfaces.

It is important to understand that each enumeration constant is an object of its enumeration type. Thus, when you define a constructor for an **enum**, the constructor is called when each enumeration constant is created. Also, each enumeration constant has its own copy of any instance variables defined by the enumeration. For example, consider the following version of **Apple**:

```
// Use an enum constructor, instance variable, and method.
enum Apple {
  Jonathan(10), GoldenDel(9), RedDel(12), Winesap(15), Cortland(8);

  private int price; // price of each apple

  // Constructor
  Apple(int p) { price = p; }

  int getPrice() { return price; }
```

```
}

class EnumDemo3 {
  public static void main(String args[])
  {
    Apple ap;

    // Display price of Winesap.
    System.out.println("Winesap costs " +
                       Apple.Winesap.getPrice() +
                       " cents.\n");

    // Display all apples and prices.
    System.out.println("All apple prices:");
    for(Apple a : Apple.values())
      System.out.println(a + " costs " + a.getPrice() +
                         " cents.");
  }
}
```

The output is shown here:

```
Winesap costs 15 cents.

All apple prices:
Jonathan costs 10 cents.
GoldenDel costs 9 cents.
RedDel costs 12 cents.
Winesap costs 15 cents.
Cortland costs 8 cents.
```

This version of **Apple** adds three things. The first is the instance variable **price**, which is used to hold the price of each variety of apple. The second is the **Apple** constructor, which is passed the price of an apple. The third is the method **getPrice( )**, which returns the value of **price**.

When the variable **ap** is declared in **main( )**, the constructor for **Apple** is called once for each constant that is specified. Notice how the arguments to the constructor are specified, by putting them inside parentheses, after each constant, as shown here:

```
Jonathan(10), GoldenDel(9), RedDel(12), Winesap(15), Cortland(8);
```

These values are passed to the **p** parameter of **Apple( )**, which then assigns this value to **price**. Again, the constructor is called once for each constant.

Because each enumeration constant has its own copy of **price**, you can obtain the price of a specified type of apple by calling **getPrice( )**. For example, in **main( )** the price of a Winesap is obtained by the following call:

```
Apple.Winesap.getPrice()
```

The prices of all varieties are obtained by cycling through the enumeration using a **for** loop. Because there is a copy of **price** for each enumeration constant, the value associated with one constant is separate and distinct from the value associated with another constant. This is a powerful concept, which is only available when enumerations are implemented as classes, as Java does.

Although the preceding example contains only one constructor, an **enum** can offer two or more overloaded forms, just as can any other class. For example, this version of **Apple** provides a default constructor that initializes the price to −1, to indicate that no price data is available:

```
// Use an enum constructor.
enum Apple {
   Jonathan(10), GoldenDel(9), RedDel, Winesap(15), Cortland(8);

   private int price; // price of each apple

   // Constructor
   Apple(int p) { price = p; }

   // Overloaded constructor
   Apple() { price = -1; }

   int getPrice() { return price; }
}
```

Notice that in this version, **RedDel** is not given an argument. This means that the default constructor is called, and **RedDel**'s price variable is given the value −1.

Here are two restrictions that apply to enumerations. First, an enumeration can't inherit another class. Second, an **enum** cannot be a superclass. This means that an **enum** can't be extended. Otherwise, **enum** acts much like any other class type. The key is to remember that each of the enumeration constants are objects of the class in which they are defined.

Enumerations Inherit Enum

Although you can't inherit a superclass when declaring an **enum**, all enumerations automatically inherit one: **java.lang.Enum**. **Enum** is a generic class that is declared as shown here:

abstract class Enum<E extends Enum<E>>

Here, **E** stands for the enumeration type. **Enum** has no public constructors. **Enum** defines several methods, shown in Table 6-1, that are available for use by all enumerations. For the most part, **Enum**'s methods are easy to understand, but four warrant a closer look.

Method	Description
protected final Object clone( ) throws CloneNotSupportedException	Invoking this method causes a **CloneNotSupportedException** to be thrown. This prevents enumerations from being cloned.
final int compareTo(E e)	Compares the ordinal value of two constants of the same enumeration. Returns a negative value if the invoking constant has an ordinal value less than e's, zero if the two ordinal values are the same, and a positive value if the invoking constant has an ordinal value greater than e's.
final boolean equals(Object obj)	Returns true if obj and the invoking object refer to the same constant.
final Class<E> getDeclaringClass( )	Returns the type of the enumeration of which the invoking constant is a member.
final int hashCode( )	Returns the hash code for the invoking object.
final String name( )	Returns the unaltered name of the invoking constant.
final int ordinal( )	Returns a value that indicates an enumeration constant's position in the list of constants.
String toString( )	Returns the name of the invoking constant. This name may differ from the one used in the enumeration's declaration.
static <T extends Enum<T>> T valueOf(Class<T> e-type, String name)	Returns the constant associated with name in the enumeration type specified by e-type.

Table 6-1   *The Methods Defined by* **Enum**

Notice that the **clone( )** method is overloaded in such a way that it simply throws a **CloneNotSupportedException**. This prevents an enumeration constant from being cloned. This ensures that there is always one and only one copy of an enumeration constant.

You can obtain a value that indicates an enumeration constant's position in the list of constants. This is called its *ordinal value,* and it is retrieved by calling the **ordinal( )** method. Ordinal values begin at zero. Thus, in the **Apple** enumeration, **Jonathan** has an ordinal value of zero, **GoldenDel** has an ordinal value of 1, **RedDel** has an ordinal value of 2, and so on.

You can compare the ordinal value of two constants of the same enumeration by using the **compareTo( )** method, shown again here for convenience:

final int compareTo(E *e*)

It is important to understand that both the invoking constant and *e* must be of the same enumeration. If they are not, a compilation error will occur. If the invoking constant has an ordinal value less than *e*'s, then **compareTo( )** returns a negative value. If the two ordinal values are the same, then zero is returned. If the invoking constant has an ordinal value greater than *e*'s, then a positive value is returned.

You can compare for equality an enumeration constant with any other object by using **equals( )**, which overrides the **equals( )** method defined by **Object**. Although **equals( )** can compare an enumeration constant to any other object, those two objects will be equal only if they both refer to the same constant, within the same enumeration. Simply having ordinal values in common will not cause **equals( )** to return true if the two constants are from different enumerations.

Remember, you can compare two enumeration references for equality by using = =.

The following program demonstrates the **ordinal( )**, **compareTo( )**, and **equals( )** methods:

```
// Demonstrate ordinal(), compareTo(), and equals().

// An enumeration of apple varieties.
enum Apple {
   Jonathan, GoldenDel, RedDel, Winesap, Cortland
}
```

```
class EnumDemo4 {
  public static void main(String args[])
  {
    Apple ap, ap2, ap3;

    // Obtain all ordinal values using ordinal().
    System.out.println("Here are all apple constants" +
                       " and their ordinal values: ");
    for(Apple a : Apple.values())
      System.out.println(a + " " + a.ordinal());

    ap =  Apple.RedDel;
    ap2 = Apple.GoldenDel;
    ap3 = Apple.RedDel;

    System.out.println();

    // Demonstrate compareTo() and equals()
    if(ap.compareTo(ap2) < 0)
      System.out.println(ap + " comes before " + ap2);

    if(ap.compareTo(ap2) > 0)
      System.out.println(ap2 + " comes before " + ap);

    if(ap.compareTo(ap3) == 0)
      System.out.println(ap + " equals " + ap3);

    System.out.println();

    if(ap.equals(ap2))
      System.out.println("Error!");

    if(ap.equals(ap3))
      System.out.println(ap + " equals " + ap3);

    if(ap == ap3)
      System.out.println(ap + " == " + ap3);

  }
}
```

The output from the program is shown here:

```
Here are all apple constants and their ordinal values:
Jonathan 0
GoldenDel 1
RedDel 2
Winesap 3
Cortland 4

GoldenDel comes before RedDel
RedDel equals RedDel

RedDel equals RedDel
RedDel == RedDel
```

CHAPTER 7

Metadata

J ava 2, v5.0 adds a powerful new facility called *metadata,* which enables you to embed supplemental information into a source file. This information, called an *annotation,* does not change the actions of a program. Thus, an annotation leaves the semantics of a program unchanged. However, this information can be used by various tools, during both development and deployment. For example, an annotation might be processed by a source-code generator. Although Sun refers to this feature as metadata, the term *program annotation facility* is also used, and is probably more descriptive.

Metadata Basics

Metadata is created through a mechanism based on the **interface**. Let's begin with an example. Here is the declaration for an annotation called **MyAnno**:

```
// A simple annotation type.
@interface MyAnno {
  String str();
  int val();
}
```

First, notice the **@** that precedes the keyword **interface**. This tells the compiler that an annotation type is being declared. Next, notice the two members **str( )** and **val( )**. All annotations consist solely of method declarations. However, you don't provide bodies for these methods. Instead, Java implements these methods. Moreover, the methods act much like fields, as you will see.

All annotation types automatically extend the **Annotation** interface. Thus, **Annotation** is a super-interface of all annotations. It is declared within the **java.lang.annotation** package. It overrides **hashCode( )**, **equals( )**, and **toString( )**, which are defined by **Object**. It also specifies **annotationType( )**, which returns a **Class** object that represents the invoking annotation.

Once you have declared an annotation, you can use it to annotate a declaration. Any type of declaration can have an annotation associated with it. For example, classes, methods, fields, parameters, and **enum** constants can be annotated. Even an annotation can be annotated. In all cases, the annotation precedes the rest of the declaration.

When you apply an annotation, you give values to its members. For example, here is an example of **MyAnno** being applied to a method:

```
// Annotate a method.
@MyAnno(str = "Annotation Example", val = 100)
public static void myMeth() { // ...
```

This annotation is linked with the method **myMeth( )**. Look closely at the annotation syntax. The name of the annotation, preceded by an **@**, is followed by a parenthesized list of member initializations. To give a member a value, that member's name is assigned a value. Therefore, in the example, the string "Annotation Example" is assigned to the **str** member of **MyAnno**. Notice that no parentheses follow **str** in this assignment. When an annotation member is given a value, only its name is used. Thus, annotation members look like fields in this context.

Specifying a Retention Policy

Before exploring metadata further, it is necessary to discuss *annotation retention policies*. A retention policy determines at what point an annotation is discarded. Java defines three such policies—**SOURCE**, **CLASS**, and **RUNTIME**—which are encapsulated within the **java.lang.annotation.RetentionPolicy** enumeration.

An annotation with a retention policy of **SOURCE** is retained only in the source file and is discarded during compilation.

An annotation with a retention policy of **CLASS** is stored in the **.class** file during compilation. However, it is not available through the JVM during run time.

An annotation with a retention policy of **RUNTIME** is stored in the **.class** file during compilation and is available through the JVM during run time. Thus, **RUNTIME** retention offers the greatest annotation persistence.

A retention policy is specified for an annotation by using one of Java's built-in annotations: **@Retention**. Its general form is shown here:

@Retention(*retention-policy*)

Here, *retention-policy* must be one of the previously discussed enumeration constants. If no retention policy is specified for an annotation, then the default policy of **CLASS** is used.

The following version of **MyAnno** uses **@Retention** to specify the **RUNTIME** retention policy. Thus, **MyAnno** will be available to the JVM during program execution.

```
@Retention(RetentionPolicy.RUNTIME)
@interface MyAnno {
  String str();
  int val();
}
```

Obtaining Annotations at Run Time by Use of Reflection

Although annotations are designed mostly for use by other development or deployment tools, they can be queried at run time by any Java program through the use of reflection. As most readers likely know, *reflection* is the feature that enables information about a class to be obtained at run time. The reflection API is contain in the **java.lang.reflect** package. There are a number of ways to use reflection, and we won't examine them all here. We will, however, walk through a few examples that apply to annotations.

The first step to using reflection is to obtain a **Class** object that represents the class whose annotations you want to obtain. There are various ways to obtain a **Class** object. One of the easiest is to call **getClass( )**, which is a method defined by **Object**. Its general form is shown here:

final Class<? extends Object> getClass( )

It returns the **Class** object that represents the invoking object. Notice that **Class** is now generic.

After you have obtained a **Class** object, you can use its methods to obtain information about the various items declared by the class, including its annotations. If you want to obtain the annotations associated with a specific item declared within a class, you must first obtain an object that represents that item. For example, **Class** supplies (among others) the **getMethod( )**, **getField( )**, and

getConstructor( ) methods, which obtain information about a method, field, and constructor, respectively. These methods return objects of type **Method**, **Field**, and **Constructor**.

To understand the process, let's work through an example that obtains the annotations associated with a method. To do this, you first obtain a **Class** object that represents the class, and then call **getMethod( )** on that **Class** object, specifying the name of the method. **getMethod( )** has this general form:

Method getMethod(String *methName*, Class ... *paramTypes*)

The name of the method is passed in *methName*. If the method has arguments, then **Class** objects representing those types must also be specified by *paramTypes*. Notice that *paramTypes* is a varargs parameter. This means that you can specify as many parameter types as needed, including zero. **getMethod( )** returns a **Method** object that represents the method. If the method can't be found, **NoSuchMethodException** is thrown.

From a **Class, Method, Field, Constructor**, or **Package** object, you can obtain a specific annotation associated with that object by calling **getAnnotation( )**. Its general form is shown here:

<T extends Annotation> T getAnnotation(Class<T> *annoType*)

Here, *annoType* is a **Class** object that represents the annotation in which you are interested. It returns a reference to the annotation. Using this reference, you can obtain the values associated with the annotation's members.

Here is a program that assembles all of the pieces shown earlier and uses reflection to display the annotation associated with a method:

```
import java.lang.annotation.*;
import java.lang.reflect.*;

// An annotation type declaration.
@Retention(RetentionPolicy.RUNTIME)
@interface MyAnno {
  String str();
  int val();
}

class Meta {
```

```
  // Annotate a method.
  @MyAnno(str = "Annotation Example", val = 100)
  public static void myMeth() {
    Meta ob = new Meta();

    // Obtain the annotation for this method
    // and display the values of the members.
    try {
      // First, get a Class object that represents
      // this class.
      Class c = ob.getClass();

      // Now, get a Method object that represents
      // this method.
      Method m = c.getMethod("myMeth");

      // Next, get the annotation for this class.
      MyAnno anno = m.getAnnotation(MyAnno.class);

      // Finally, display the values.
      System.out.println(anno.str() + " " + anno.val());
    } catch (NoSuchMethodException exc) {
       System.out.println("Method Not Found.");
    }
  }

  public static void main(String args[]) {
    myMeth();
  }
}
```

The output from the program is shown here:

```
Annotation Example 100
```

This program uses reflection as described to obtain and display the values of **str** and **val** in the **MyAnno** annotation associated with **myMeth( )** in the **Meta** class. There are two things to pay special attention to. First, in this line

```
MyAnno anno = m.getAnnotation(MyAnno.class);
```

notice the expression **MyAnno.class**. This expression evaluates to a **Class** object of type **MyAnno**, the annotation. This construct is called a *class literal.* You can use this type of expression whenever a **Class** object of a known class is needed. For example, this statement could have been used to obtain the **Class** object for **Meta**:

```
Class c = Meta.class;
```

Of course, this approach only works when you know the class name of an object in advance, which might not always be the case. In general, you can obtain a class literal for classes, interfaces, simple types, and arrays.

The second point of interest is the way the values associated with **str** and **val** are obtained when they are output by the following line:

```
System.out.println(anno.str() + " " + anno.val());
```

Notice that they are invoked using the method-call syntax. This same approach is used whenever the value of an annotation member is required.

A Second Reflection Example

In the preceding example, **myMeth( )** has no parameters. Thus, when **getMethod( )** was called, only the name **myMeth** was passed. To obtain a method that has parameters, you must specify class objects representing the types of those parameters as arguments to **getMethod( )**. For example, here is a slightly different version of the preceding program:

```
import java.lang.annotation.*;
import java.lang.reflect.*;

@Retention(RetentionPolicy.RUNTIME)
@interface MyAnno {
  String str();
  int val();
}

class Meta {

  // myMeth now has two arguments.
  @MyAnno(str = "Two Parameters", val = 19)
  public static void myMeth(String str, int i)
  {
    Meta ob = new Meta();

    try {
```

```
      Class c = ob.getClass();

      // Here, the parameter types are specified.
      Method m = c.getMethod("myMeth", String.class, int.class);

      MyAnno anno = m.getAnnotation(MyAnno.class);

      System.out.println(anno.str() + " " + anno.val());
    } catch (NoSuchMethodException exc) {
      System.out.println("Method Not Found.");
    }
  }

  public static void main(String args[]) {
    myMeth("test", 10);
  }
}
```

The output from this version is shown here:

```
Two Parameters 19
```

In this version, **myMeth( )** takes a **String** and an **int** parameter. To obtain information about this method, **getMethod( )** must be called as shown here:

```
Method m = c.getMethod("myMeth", String.class, int.class);
```

Here, the **Class** objects representing **String** and **int** are passed as additional arguments.

Obtaining All Annotations

You can obtain all annotations associated with an item by calling **getAnnotations( )** on that item. It has this general form:

> Annotation[ ] getAnnotations( )

It returns an array of the annotations. **getAnnotations( )** can be called on objects of type **Class, Method, Constructor, Field**, or **Package**.

Here is another reflection example that shows how to obtain all annotations associated with a class and with a method. It declares two annotations. It then uses those annotations to annotate a class and a method.

```
// Show all annotations for a class and a method.
import java.lang.annotation.*;
import java.lang.reflect.*;

@Retention(RetentionPolicy.RUNTIME)
@interface MyAnno {
  String str();
  int val();
}

@Retention(RetentionPolicy.RUNTIME)
@interface What {
  String description();
}

@What(description = "An annotation test class")
@MyAnno(str = "Meta2", val = 99)
class Meta2 {

  @What(description = "An annotation test method")
  @MyAnno(str = "Testing", val = 100)
  public static void myMeth() {
    Meta2 ob = new Meta2();

    try {
      Annotation annos[] = ob.getClass().getAnnotations();

      // Display all annotations for Meta2.
      System.out.println("All annotations for Meta2:");
      for(Annotation a : annos)
        System.out.println(a);

      System.out.println();

      // Display all annotations for myMeth.
      Method m = ob.getClass( ).getMethod("myMeth");
      annos = m.getAnnotations();
```

```
      System.out.println("All annotations for myMeth:");
      for(Annotation a : annos)
        System.out.println(a);

    } catch (NoSuchMethodException exc) {
      System.out.println("Method Not Found.");
    }
  }

  public static void main(String args[]) {
    myMeth();
  }
}
```

The output is shown here:

```
All annotations for Meta2:
@What(description=An annotation test class)
@MyAnno(str=Meta2, val=99)

All annotations for myMeth:
@What(description=An annotation test method)
@MyAnno(str=Testing, val=100)
```

The program uses **getAnnotations( )** to obtain an array of all annotations associated with the **Meta2** class and with the **myMeth( )** method. As explained, **getAnnotations( )** returns an array of **Annotation** objects. Recall that **Annotation** is a super-interface of all annotation interfaces and that it overrides **equals( )** and **toString( )** in **Object**. Thus, when a reference to an **Annotation** is output, its **toString( )** method is called to generate a string that describes the annotation, as the preceding output shows.

The AnnotatedElement Interface

The methods **getAnnotation( )** and **getAnnotations( )** used by the preceding examples are defined by the new **AnnotatedElement** interface, which is defined in **java.lang.reflect**. This interface supports reflection for annotations and is implemented by the classes **Method**, **Field**, **Constructor**, **Class**, and **Package**. **AnnotatedElement** defines the methods shown in Table 7-1. Therefore, these methods are available to any object to which annotations can be applied.

Method	Description
<T extends Annotation> T getAnnotation(Class<T> *annoType*)	Returns the annotation of type *annoType* associated with the invoking object.
Annotation[ ] getAnnotations( )	Returns an array containing all annotations associated with the invoking object.
Annotation[ ] getDeclaredAnnotations( )	Returns an array containing all noninherited annotations associated with the invoking object.
boolean isAnnotationPresent(Class<? extends Annotation> *annoType*)	Returns true if an annotation specified by *annoType* is associated with the invoking object. It returns false otherwise.

Table 7-1   *The Methods Defined by **AnnotatedElement***

Using Default Values

You can give annotation members default values that will be used if no value is specified when the annotation is applied. A default value is specified by adding a **default** clause to a member's declaration. It has this general form:

> *type member*( ) default *value*;

Here, *value* must be of a type compatible with *type*.

Here is **@MyAnno** rewritten to include default values:

```
// An annotation type declaration that includes defaults.
@Retention(RetentionPolicy.RUNTIME)
@interface MyAnno {
  String str() default "Testing";
  int val() default 9000;
}
```

This declaration gives a default value of "Testing" to **str** and 9000 to **val**. This means that neither value needs to be specified when **@MyAnno** is used. However, either or both can be given values if desired. Therefore, following are the four ways that **@MyAnno** can be used:

```
@MyAnno() // both str and val default
@MyAnno(str = "some string") // val defaults
@MyAnno(val = 100) // str defaults
@MyAnno(str = "Testing", val = 100) // no defaults
```

The following program demonstrates the use of default values in an annotation:

```
import java.lang.annotation.*;
import java.lang.reflect.*;

// An annotation type declaration that includes defaults.
@Retention(RetentionPolicy.RUNTIME)
@interface MyAnno {
  String str() default "Testing";
  int val() default 9000;
}

class Meta3 {

  // Annotate a method using the default values.
  @MyAnno()
  public static void myMeth() {
    Meta3 ob = new Meta3();

    // Obtain the annotation for this method
    // and display the values of the members.
    try {
      Class c = ob.getClass();

      Method m = c.getMethod("myMeth");

      MyAnno anno = m.getAnnotation(MyAnno.class);

      System.out.println(anno.str() + " " + anno.val());
    } catch (NoSuchMethodException exc) {
        System.out.println("Method Not Found.");
    }
  }

  public static void main(String args[]) {
    myMeth();
  }
}
```

The output is shown here:

```
Testing 9000
```

Marker Annotations

A *marker* annotation is a special kind of annotation that contains no members. Its sole purpose is to mark a declaration. Thus, its presence as an annotation is sufficient. The best way to determine if a marker annotation is present is to use the method **isAnnotationPresent( )**, which is defined by the **AnnotatedElement** interface. Thus, it is available in **Class, Field, Method, Constructor**, and **Package**.

Here is an example that uses a marker annotation. It uses **isAnnotationPresent( )** to determine if the marker is present. Because a marker interface contains no members, simply determining its existence is sufficient.

```
import java.lang.annotation.*;
import java.lang.reflect.*;

// A marker annotation.
@Retention(RetentionPolicy.RUNTIME)
@interface MyMarker { }

class Marker {

  // Annotate a method using a marker.
  // Notice that no ( ) is needed.
  @MyMarker
  public static void myMeth() {
    Marker ob = new Marker();

    try {
      Method m = ob.getClass().getMethod("myMeth");

      // Determine if the annotation is present.
      if(m.isAnnotationPresent(MyMarker.class))
        System.out.println("MyMarker is present.");

    } catch (NoSuchMethodException exc) {
      System.out.println("Method Not Found.");
    }
  }

  public static void main(String args[]) {
    myMeth();
  }
}
```

The output, shown here, confirms that **@MyMarker** is present:

```
MyMarker is present.
```

In the program, notice that you do not need to follow **@MyMarker** with parentheses when it is applied. Thus **MyMarker** is applied simply by using its name, like this:

> @MyMarker

It is not wrong to supply an empty set of parentheses, but they are not needed.

Single-Member Annotations

A *single-member* annotation is another special kind of annotation. It contains only one member. It works like a normal annotation except that it allows a shorthand form of specifying the value of the member. When only one member is present, you can simply specify the value for that member when the annotation is applied; you don't need to specify the name of the member. However, in order to use this shorthand, the name of the member must be **value**.

Here is an example that creates and uses a single-member annotation:

```
import java.lang.annotation.*;
import java.lang.reflect.*;

// A single-member annotation.
@Retention(RetentionPolicy.RUNTIME)
@interface MySingle {
  int value(); // this variable name must be value
}

class Single {

  // Annotate a method using a marker.
  @MySingle(100)
  public static void myMeth() {
    Single ob = new Single();

    try {
```

```
    Method m = ob.getClass().getMethod("myMeth");

    MySingle anno = m.getAnnotation(MySingle.class);

    System.out.println(anno.value()); // displays 100

  } catch (NoSuchMethodException exc) {
    System.out.println("Method Not Found.");
  }
}

public static void main(String args[]) {
  myMeth();
}
}
```

As expected, this program displays the value 100. In the program, **@MySingle** is used to annotate **myMeth( )**, as shown here:

```
@MySingle(100)
```

Notice that **value =** need not be specified.

You can use the single-value syntax when applying an annotation that has other members, but those other members must all have default values. For example, here the value **xyz** is added, with a default value of zero:

```
@interface SomeAnno {
  int value();
  int xyz() default 0;
}
```

In cases in which you want to use the default for **xyz**, you can apply **@SomeAnno**, as shown next, by simply specifying the value of **value** by using the single-member syntax:

```
@SomeAnno(88)
```

In this case, **xyz** defaults to zero, and **value** gets the value 88. Of course, to specify a different value for **xyz** requires that both members be explicitly named, as shown here:

```
@SomeAnno(value = 88, xyz = 99)
```

Remember, whenever you are using a single-member annotation, the name of that member must be **value**.

The Built-In Annotations

Java defines seven built-in annotations. Four are imported from **java.lang.annotation**: **@Retention**, **@Documented**, **@Target**, and **@Inherited**. Three, **@Override**, **@Deprecated**, and **@SuppressWarnings**, are included in **java.lang**. Each is described here.

@Retention

@Retention is designed to be used only as an annotation to another annotation. It specifies the retention policy as described earlier in this chapter.

@Documented

The **@Documented** annotation is a marker interface that tells a tool that an annotation is to be documented. It is designed to be used only as an annotation to an annotation declaration.

@Target

The **@Target** annotation specifies the types of declarations to which an annotation can be applied. It is designed to be used only as an annotation to another annotation. **@Target** takes one argument, which must be a constant from the **ElementType** enumeration. This argument specifies the types of declarations to which the annotation can be applied. The constants are shown here along with the type of declaration to which they correspond:

Target Constant	Annotation Can Be Applied To
ANNOTATION_TYPE	Another annotation
CONSTRUCTOR	Constructor
FIELD	Field

Target Constant	Annotation Can Be Applied To
LOCAL_VARIABLE	Local variable
METHOD	Method
PACKAGE	Package
PARAMETER	Parameter
TYPE	Class, interface, or enumeration

You can specify one or more of these values in a **@Target** annotation. To specify multiple values, you must specify them within a braces-delimited list. For example, to specify that an annotation applies only to fields and local variables, you can use this **@Target** annotation:

```
@Target( { ElementType.FIELD, ElementType.LOCAL_VARIABLE } )
```

@Inherited

@Inherited is a marker annotation that can be used only on another annotation declaration. Furthermore, it affects only annotations that will be used on class declarations. **@Inherited** causes the annotation for a superclass to be inherited by a subclass. Therefore, when a request for a specific annotation is made to the subclass, if that annotation is not present in the subclass, then its superclass is checked. If that annotation is present in the superclass, and if it is annotated with **@Inherited**, then that annotation will be returned.

@Override

@Override is a marker annotation that can be used only on methods. A method annotated with **@Override** must override a method from a superclass. If it doesn't, a compile-time error will result. It is used to ensure that a superclass method is actually overridden, and not simply overloaded.

@Deprecated

@Deprecated is a marker annotation. It indicates that a declaration is obsolete and has been replaced by a newer form.

@SuppressWarnings

@SuppressWarnings specifies that one or more warnings that might be issued by the compiler are to be suppressed. The warnings to suppress are specified by name, in string form. This annotation can be applied to any type of declaration.

Some Restrictions

There are a number of restrictions that apply to annotation declarations. First, no annotation can inherit another. Second, all methods declared by an annotation must be without parameters. Furthermore, they must return one of the following:

- A simple type, such as **int** or **double**
- An object of type **String** or **Class**
- An **enum** type
- Another annotation type
- An array of one of the preceding types

Annotations cannot be generic. In other words, they cannot take type parameters. Finally, they cannot specify a **throws** clause.

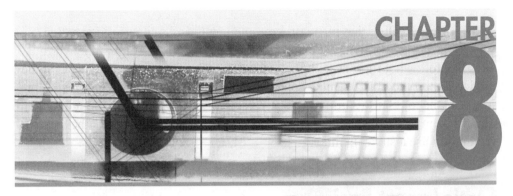

Static Import

A new feature that many programmers will find quite useful is called *static import* and it expands the capabilities of the **import** keyword. By following **import** with the keyword **static**, an **import** statement can be used to import the static members of a class or interface. When using static import, it is possible to refer to static members directly by their names, without having to qualify them by the name of their class. This simplifies and shortens the syntax required to use a static member.

Static Import Basics

To understand the usefulness of static import, let's begin with an example that *does not* use it. The following program computes the hypotenuse of a right triangle. It uses two static methods from Java's built-in math class **Math**, which is part of **java.lang**. The first is **Math.pow( )**, which returns a value raised to a specified power. The second is **Math.sqrt( )**, which returns the square root of its argument.

```
// Compute the hypotenuse of a right triangle.
class Hypot {
  public static void main(String args[]) {
    double side1, side2;
    double hypot;

    side1 = 3.0;
    side2 = 4.0;

    // Notice how sqrt() and pow() must be qualified by
    // their class name, which is Math.
    hypot = Math.sqrt(Math.pow(side1, 2) +
                      Math.pow(side2, 2));

    System.out.println("Given sides of lengths " +
                       side1 + " and " + side2 +
                       " the hypotenuse is " +
                       hypot);
  }
}
```

Because **pow( )** and **sqrt( )** are static methods, they must be called through the use of their class name, **Math**. This results in a somewhat unwieldy hypotenuse calculation:

```
hypot = Math.sqrt(Math.pow(side1, 2) +
                  Math.pow(side2, 2));
```

As this simple example illustrates, having to specify the class name each time **pow( )** or **sqrt( )** (or any of Java's other math methods, such as **sin( )**, **cos( )**, and **tan( )**) is used can grow tedious.

You can eliminate the tedium of specifying the class name through the use of static import, as shown in the following version of the preceding program:

```
// Use static import to bring sqrt() and pow() into view.
import static java.lang.Math.sqrt;
import static java.lang.Math.pow;

// Compute the hypotenuse of a right triangle.
class Hypot {
  public static void main(String args[]) {
    double side1, side2;
    double hypot;

    side1 = 3.0;
    side2 = 4.0;

    // Here, sqrt() and pow() can be called by themselves,
    // without their class name.
    hypot = sqrt(pow(side1, 2) + pow(side2, 2));

    System.out.println("Given sides of lengths " +
                       side1 + " and " + side2 +
                       " the hypotenuse is " +
                       hypot);
  }
}
```

In this version, the names **sqrt** and **pow** are brought into view by these static import statements:

```
import static java.lang.Math.sqrt;
import static java.lang.Math.pow;
```

After these statements, it is no longer necessary to qualify **sqrt( )** and **pow( )** with their class name. Therefore, the hypotenuse calculation can more conveniently be specified, as shown here:

```
hypot = sqrt(pow(side1, 2) + pow(side2, 2));
```

As you can see, this form is considerably more readable.

The General Form of Static Import

There are two general forms of the **import static** statement. The first, which is used by the preceding example, brings into view a single name. Its general form is shown here:

import static *pkg.type-name.static-member-name*;

Here, *type-name* is the name of a class or interface that contains the desired static member. Its full package name is specified by *pkg*. The name of the member is specified by *static-member-name*.

The second form of static import imports all static members. Its general form is shown here:

import static *pkg.type-name*.*;

If you will be using many static methods or fields defined by a class, then this form lets you bring them into view without having to specify each individually. Therefore, the preceding program could have used this single **import** statement to bring both **pow( )** and **sqrt( )** (and *all other* static members of **Math**) into view:

```
import static java.lang.Math.*;
```

Of course, static import is not limited to just the **Math** class or just to methods. For example, this brings the static field **System.out** into view:

```
import static java.lang.System.out;
```

After this statement, you can output to the console without having to qualify **out** with **System**, as shown here:

```
out.println("After importing System.out, you can use out directly.");
```

Whether importing **System.out** as just shown is a good idea is subject to debate. Although it does shorten the statement, it is no longer instantly clear to anyone reading the program that the **out** being referred to is **System.out**.

Importing Static Members of Classes You Create

In addition to importing the static members of classes and interfaces defined by the Java API, you can also use static import to import the static members of classes and interfaces that you create. For example, consider the **Msg** class shown here. Notice that it is contained in a package called **MyMsg**.

```
package MyMsg;

public class Msg {
  public static final int UPPER = 1;
  public static final int LOWER = 2;
  public static final int MIXED = 3;

  private String msg;

  // Display a message in the specified case.
  public void showMsg(int how) {
    String str;

    switch(how) {
      case UPPER:
        str = msg.toUpperCase();
        break;
      case LOWER:
        str = msg.toLowerCase();
        break;
      case MIXED:
        str = msg;
        break;
      default:
        System.out.println("Invalid command.");
        return;
    }

    System.out.println(str);
  }

  public Msg(String s) { msg = s; }
}
```

Msg encapsulates a string that can be displayed in its original, mixed-case form, uppercase, or lowercase, based on what value is passed to **showMsg( )**. The values that determine which case is used are **static final** integers called **UPPER**, **LOWER**, and **MIXED**. Normally, these members would need to be qualified with their class name, as in **Msg.UPPER**. For example, assuming an **Msg** object called **m**, to display the string in lowercase, you would normally call **showMsg( )** like this:

```
m.showMsg(Msg.LOWER);
```

However, if you statically import these values, you can use them directly, as in

```
m.showMsg(LOWER);
```

The following class demonstrates the process by importing the static members of **MyMsg.Msg** and then using the **LOWER**, **UPPER**, and **MIXED** constants without qualification:

```
// Static import user-defined static fields.
import MyMsg.*;

import static MyMsg.Msg.*;

class Test {
  public static void main(String args[]) {
    Msg m = new Msg("Testing static import.");

    m.showMsg(MIXED);
    m.showMsg(LOWER);
    m.showMsg(UPPER);
  }
}
```

Ambiguity

You must be careful not to create an ambiguous situation when using the static import facility. If two classes or interfaces both use the same name for a static member, and if both of these classes or interfaces are imported into the same compilation unit, then the compiler does not know which name to select when that name is used without its class qualification. For example, assume that the

MyMsg package from the preceding example also includes the following class, which also declares a static field called **UPPER**:

```
package MyMsg;

public class X {
  public static final int UPPER = 11;
  // ...
}
```

If the static members of this class are imported into a program that also imports the static members of **Msg**, then there will be ambiguity when the identifier **UPPER** is encountered. For example, given these two static imports,

```
import static MyMsg.Msg.*;
import static MyMsg.X.*;
```

does the unqualified name **UPPER** refer to **Msg.UPPER** or to **X.UPPER**? The compiler has no way to know and, therefore, reports an ambiguity error.

A Word of Warning

As convenient as static import can be, it is important not to abuse it. Remember, the reason that Java organizes its libraries into packages is to avoid namespace collisions. When you import static members, you are bringing those members into the global namespace. Thus, you are increasing the potential for namespace conflicts, ambiguity, and the inadvertent hiding of other names. If you are using a static member once or twice in the program, it's best not to import it. Also, some static names, such as **System.out**, are so recognizable that you might not want to import them. Static import is designed for those situations in which you are using a static member repeatedly, such as when performing a series of mathematical computations. In essence, you should use, but not abuse, this feature.

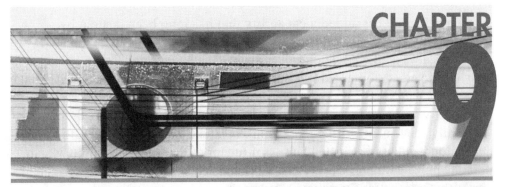

Formatted I/O

J ava 2, v5.0 has added a capability that has long been desired by programmers: the ability to easily create formatted output. Although Java has always offered a rich and varied API, it has not previously offered an easy way to create formatted text output, especially for numeric values. Although classes such as **NumberFormat**, **DateFormat**, and **MessageFormat** provided by earlier versions of Java do provide useful formatting capabilities, they are not especially convenient. Furthermore, unlike C and C++, which support the widely understood and used **printf( )** family of functions that offers a simple way to format output, Java previously has not offered such methods. One reason for this is that printf-style formatting requires the use of variable-length arguments (varargs), which Java did not support until the release of Java 2, v5.0. Once varargs were available, it was a simple matter to add a general-purpose formatter.

Java 2, v5.0 also adds support for reading formatted input. Although it has always been possible to read formatted input, it required more effort than most programmers would prefer. Now it is easy to read all types of numeric values, strings, and other types of data, whether it comes from a disk file, the keyboard, or another source.

Formatting Output with Formatter

At the core of Java's support for creating formatted output is the **Formatter** class, packaged in **java.util**. It provides *format conversions* that let you display numbers, strings, and time and date in virtually any format you like. It operates in a manner similar to the C/C++ **printf( )** function, which means that if you are familiar with C/C++, then learning to use **Formatter** will be very easy. It also further streamlines the conversion of C/C++ code to Java. If you are not familiar with C/C++, it is still quite easy to format data.

In addition to **Formatter**, Java 2, v5.0 also adds the **printf( )** method to the **PrintStream** and **PrintWriter** classes. The **printf( )** method automatically uses **Formatter** and offers a nearly one-to-one equivalence with the C/C++ **printf( )** facility, thus further facilitating the conversion of C/C++ code to Java.

NOTE

*Although Java's **Formatter** class and **printf( )** method operate in a manner very similar to the C/C++ **printf( )** function, there are some differences, and some new features. Therefore, if you come with a C/C++ background, a careful reading is advised.*

The Formatter Constructors

Before you can use **Formatter** to format output, you must create a **Formatter** object. In general, **Formatter** works by converting the binary form of data used by a program into formatted text. It stores the formatted text in a buffer, the contents of which can be obtained by your program whenever it is needed. It is possible to let **Formatter** supply this buffer automatically, or you can specify the buffer explicitly when a **Formatter** object is created. It is also possible to have **Formatter** output its buffer to a file.

The **Formatter** class defines many constructors, which enable you to construct a **Formatter** in a variety of ways. Here is a sampling:

> Formatter( )
>
> Formatter(Appendable *buf*)
>
> Formatter(Appendable *buf*, Locale *loc*)
>
> Formatter(String *filename*)
>   throws FileNotFoundException
>
> Formatter(String *filename*, String *charset*)
>   throws FileNotFoundException, UnsupportedEncodingException
>
> Formatter(File *outF*)
>   throws FileNotFoundException
>
> Formatter(OutputStream *outStrm*)

Here, *buf* specifies a buffer for the formatted output. If *buf* is null, then **Formatter** automatically allocates a **StringBuilder** to hold the formatted output. The *loc* parameter specifies a locale. If no locale is specified, the default locale is used. The *filename* parameter specifies the name of a file that will receive the formatted output. The *charset* parameter specifies the character set. If no character set is specified, then the default character set is used. The *outF* parameter specifies a reference to an open file that will receive output. The *outStrm* parameter specifies a reference to an output stream that will receive output. When using a file, output is also written to the file.

Perhaps the most widely used constructor is the first listed, which has no parameters. It automatically uses the default locale and allocates a **StringBuilder** to hold the formatted output.

The Formatter Methods

Formatter defines the methods shown in Table 9-1.

Formatting Basics

After you have created a **Formatter**, you can use it to create a formatted string. To do so, use the **format( )** method. The most commonly used version is shown here:

> Formatter format(String *fmtString*, Object ... *args*)

Method	Description
void close( )	Closes the invoking **Formatter**. This causes any resources used by the object to be released. After a **Formatter** has been closed, it cannot be reused. An attempt to use a closed **Formatter** results in a **FormatterClosedException**.
void flush( )	Flushes the format buffer. This causes any output currently in the buffer to be written to the destination. This applies mostly to a **Formatter** tied to a file.
Formatter format(String *fmtString*, Object ... *args*)	Formats the arguments passed via *args* according to the format specifiers contained in *fmtString*. Returns the invoking object.
Formatter format(Locale *loc*, String *fmtString*, Object ... *args*)	Formats the arguments passed via *args* according to the format specifiers contained in *fmtString*. The locale specified by *loc* is used for this format. Returns the invoking object.
IOException ioException( )	If the underlying object that is the destination for output throws an **IOException**, then this exception is returned. Otherwise, null is returned.
Locale locale( )	Returns the invoking object's locale.
Appendable out( )	Returns a reference to the underlying object that is the destination for output.
String toString( )	Returns a **String** containing the formatted output.

Table 9-1 *The Methods Defined by* **Formatter**

The *fmtString* consists of two types of items. The first type is composed of characters that are simply copied to the output buffer. The second type contains *format specifiers* that define the way the subsequent arguments are displayed.

In its simplest form, a format specifier begins with a percent sign followed by the format *conversion specifier*. All format conversion specifiers consist of a single character. For example, the format specifier for floating-point data is **%f**. In general, there must be the same number of arguments as there are format specifiers, and the format specifiers and the arguments are matched in order from left to right. For example, consider this fragment:

```
Formatter fmt = new Formatter();
fmt.format("Formatting %s is easy %d %f", "with Java", 10, 98.6);
```

This sequence creates a **Formatter** that contains the following string:

```
Formatting with Java is easy 10 98.600000
```

In this example, the format specifiers, **%s**, **%d**, and **%f**, are replaced with the arguments that follow the format string. Thus, the **%s** is replaced by "with Java", the **%d** is replaced by 10, and the **%f** is replaced by 98.6. All other characters are simply used as-is. As you might guess, the format specifier **%s** specifies a string, and **%d** specifies an integer value. As mentioned earlier, the **%f** specifies a floating-point value.

The **format( )** method accepts a wide variety of format specifiers, which are shown in Table 9-2. Notice that many specifiers have both upper- and lowercase forms. When an uppercase specifier is used, then letters are shown in uppercase. Otherwise, the upper- and lowercase specifiers perform the same conversion. It is important to understand that Java type-checks each format specifier against its corresponding argument. If the argument doesn't match, an **IllegalFormatException** is thrown.

Once you have formatted a string, you can obtain it by calling **toString( )**. For example, continuing with the preceding example, the following statement obtains the formatted string contained in **fmt**:

```
String str = fmt.toString();
```

Of course, if you simply want to display the formatted string, there is no reason to first assign it to a **String** object. When a **Formatter** object is passed to **println( )**, for example, its **toString( )** method is automatically called.

Format Specifier	Conversion Applied
%a %A	Floating-point hexadecimal
%b %B	Boolean
%c %C	Character
%d	Decimal integer
%h %H	Hash code of the argument
%e %E	Scientific notation
%f	Decimal floating point
%g %G	Uses **%e** or **%f**, whichever is shorter
%o	Octal integer
%n	Inserts a newline character
%s %S	String
%t %T	Time and date
%x	Integer hexadecimal
%%	Inserts a % sign

Table 9-2   *The Format Specifiers*

Here is a short program that puts together all of the pieces, showing how to create and display a formatted string:

```
// A very simple example that uses Formatter.
import java.util.*;

class FormatDemo {
  public static void main(String args[]) {
    Formatter fmt = new Formatter();

    fmt.format("Formatting %s is easy %d %f", "with Java", 10, 98.6);
```

```
      System.out.println(fmt);
    }
  }
```

One other point: You can obtain a reference to the underlying output buffer by calling **out( )**. It returns a reference to an **Appendable** object. The **Appendable** interface was added by Java 2, v5.0.

Now that you know the general mechanism used to create a formatted string, the remainder of this section discusses in detail each conversion. It also describes various options, such as justification, minimum field width, and precision.

Formatting Strings and Characters

To format an individual character, use **%c**. This causes the matching character argument to be output, unmodified. To format a string, use **%s**.

Formatting Numbers

To format an integer in decimal format, use **%d**. To format a floating-point value in decimal format, use **%f**. To format a floating-point value in scientific notation, use **%e**. Numbers represented in scientific notation take this general form:

$$x.ddddde+/-yy$$

The **%g** format specifier causes **Formatter** to use either **%f** or **%e**, whichever is shorter. The following program demonstrates the effect of the **%g** format specifier:

```
// Demonstrate the %g format specifier.
import java.util.*;

class FormatDemo2 {
  public static void main(String args[]) {
    Formatter fmt = new Formatter();

    for(double i=1000; i < 1.0e+10; i *= 100) {
      fmt.format("%g ", i);
      System.out.println(fmt);
    }

  }
}
```

It produces the following output:

```
1000.000000
1000.000000 100000.000000
1000.000000 100000.000000 1.000000e+07
1000.000000 100000.000000 1.000000e+07 1.000000e+09
```

You can display integers in octal or hexadecimal format by using **%o** and **%x**, respectively. For example, this fragment

```
fmt.format("Hex: %x, Octal: %o", 196, 196);
```

produces this output:

```
Hex: c4, Octal: 304
```

You can display floating-point values in hexadecimal format by using **%a**. The format produced by **%a** appears a bit strange at first glance. This is because its representation uses a form similar to scientific notation that consists of a significand and an exponent, both in hexadecimal. Here is the general format:

0x1.*sigpexp*

Here, *sig* contains the fractional portion of the significand and *exp* contains the exponent. The **p** indicates the start of the exponent. For example, this call

```
fmt.format("%a", 123.123);
```

produces this output:

```
0x1.ec7df3b645a1dp6
```

Formatting Time and Date

One of the more powerful conversion specifiers is **%t**. It lets you format time and date information. The **%t** specifier works a bit differently than the others because it requires the use of a suffix to describe the portion and precise format of the time or date desired. The suffixes are shown in Table 9-3. For example, to display minutes, you would use **%tM**, where **M** indicates minutes in a two-character field. The argument corresponding to the **%t** specifier must be of type **Calendar**, **Date**, **Long**, or **long**.

Suffix	Replaced By
a	Abbreviated weekday name
A	Full weekday name
b	Abbreviated month name
B	Full month name
c	Standard date and time string formatted as day month date hh::mm:ss tzone year
C	First two digits of year
d	Day of month as a decimal (01 to 31)
D	month/day/year
e	Day of month as a decimal (1 to 31)
F	year-month-day
h	Abbreviated month name
H	Hour (00 to 23)
I	Hour (01 to 12)
j	Day of year as a decimal (001 to 366)
k	Hour (0 to 23)
l	Hour (1 to 12)
L	Millisecond (000 to 999)
m	Month as decimal (01 to 13)
M	Minute as decimal (00 to 59)
N	Nanosecond (000000000 to 999999999)
P	Locale's equivalent of AM or PM in uppercase
p	Locale's equivalent of AM or PM in lowercase
Q	Milliseconds from 1/1/1970
r	hh:mm (12-hour format)
R	hh:mm (24-hour format)
S	Seconds (00 to 60)
s	Seconds from 1/1/1970 UTC
T	hh:mm:ss (24-hour format)
y	Year in decimal without century (00 to 99)
Y	Year in decimal including century (0001 to 9999)
z	Offset from UTC
Z	Time zone name

Table 9-3   *The Time and Date Format Suffixes*

Here is a program that demonstrates several of the formats:

```java
// Formatting time and date.
import java.util.*;

class TimeDateFormat {
  public static void main(String args[]) {
    Formatter fmt = new Formatter();
    Calendar cal = Calendar.getInstance();

    // Display standard 12-hour time format.
    fmt.format("%tr", cal);
    System.out.println(fmt);

    // Display complete time and date information.
    fmt = new Formatter();
    fmt.format("%tc", cal);
    System.out.println(fmt);

    // Display just hour and minute.
    fmt = new Formatter();
    fmt.format("%tl:%tM", cal, cal);
    System.out.println(fmt);

    // Display month by name and number.
    fmt = new Formatter();
    fmt.format("%tB %tb %tm", cal, cal, cal);
    System.out.println(fmt);
  }
}
```

Sample output is shown here:

```
09:17:15 AM
Sun Dec 12 09:17:15 CST 2004
9:17
December Dec 12
```

The %n and %% Specifiers

The **%n** and **%%** format specifiers differ from the others in that they do not match an argument. Instead, they are simply escape sequences that insert a character into the output sequence. The **%n** inserts a newline. The **%%** inserts a percent sign. Neither of these characters can be entered directly into the format string. Of course, you can also use the standard escape sequence \n to embed a newline character.

Here is an example that demonstrates the **%n** and **%%** format specifiers:

```
// Demonstrate the %n and %% format specifiers.
import java.util.*;

class FormatDemo3 {
  public static void main(String args[]) {
    Formatter fmt = new Formatter();

    fmt.format("Copying file%nTransfer is %d%% complete", 88);
    System.out.println(fmt);
  }
}
```

It displays the following output:

```
Copying file
Transfer is 88% complete
```

Specifying a Minimum Field Width

An integer placed between the % sign and the format conversion code acts as a *minimum field width specifier.* This pads the output with spaces to ensure that it reaches a certain minimum length. If the string or number is longer than that minimum, it will still be printed in full. The default padding is done with spaces. If you want to pad with 0's, place a 0 before the field width specifier. For example, **%05d** will pad a number of less than five digits with 0's so that its total length is five digits. The field width specifier can be used with all format specifiers except **%n**.

The following program demonstrates the minimum field width specifier by applying it to the **%f** conversion:

```
// Demonstrate a field width specifier.
import java.util.*;

class FormatDemo4 {
  public static void main(String args[]) {
```

```
Formatter fmt = new Formatter();

fmt.format("|%f|%n|%12f|%n|%012f|",
           10.12345, 10.12345, 10.12345);

System.out.println(fmt);


  }
}
```

Its output is shown here:

```
|10.123450|
|   10.123450|
|00010.123450|
```

The first line displays the number 10.12345 in its default width. The second line displays that value in a 12-character field. The third line displays the value in a 12-character field, padded with leading zeros.

   The minimum field width specifier is often used to produce tables in which the columns line up. For example, the next program produces a table of squares and cubes for the numbers between 1 and 10:

```
// Create a table of squares and cubes.
import java.util.*;

class FieldWidthDemo {
  public static void main(String args[]) {
    Formatter fmt;

    for(int i=1; i <= 10; i++) {
      fmt = new Formatter();

      fmt.format("%4d %4d %4d", i, i*i, i*i*i);
      System.out.println(fmt);
    }

  }
}
```

This program produces the following output.

```
 1    1    1
 2    4    8
 3    9   27
 4   16   64
 5   25  125
 6   36  216
 7   49  343
 8   64  512
 9   81  729
10  100 1000
```

Specifying Precision

A *precision specifier* can be applied to the **%f, %e, %g,** and **%s** format specifiers. It follows the minimum field width specifier (if there is one) and consists of a period followed by an integer. Its exact meaning depends upon the type of data to which it is applied.

When you apply the precision specifier to floating-point data using the **%f, %e,** or **%g** specifiers, it determines the number of decimal places displayed. For example, **%10.4f** displays a number at least ten characters wide with four decimal places. The default precision is 6.

Applied to strings, the precision specifier specifies the maximum field length. For example, **%5.7s** displays a string at least five and not exceeding seven characters long. If the string is longer than the maximum field width, the end characters will be truncated.

The following program illustrates the precision specifier:

```java
// Demonstrate the precision specifier.
import java.util.*;

class PrecisionDemo {
  public static void main(String args[]) {
    Formatter fmt = new Formatter();

    // Format 4 decimal places.
    fmt.format("%.4f", 123.1234567);
    System.out.println(fmt);

    // Format to 2 decimal places in a 16-character field.
    fmt = new Formatter();
```

```
    fmt.format("%16.2e", 123.1234567);
    System.out.println(fmt);

    // Display at most 15 characters in a string.
    fmt = new Formatter();
    fmt.format("%.15s", "Formatting with Java is now easy.");
    System.out.println(fmt);
  }
}
```

It produces the following output:

```
123.1235
        1.23e+02
Formatting with
```

Using the Format Flags

Formatter recognizes a set of format *flags* that let you control various aspects of a conversion. All format flags are single characters, and a format flag follows the **%** in a format specification. The flags are shown here:

Flag	Effect
–	Left justification
#	Alternate conversion format
0	Output is padded with zeros rather than spaces
space	Positive numeric output is preceded by a space
+	Positive numeric output is preceded by a + sign
,	Numeric values include grouping separators
(	Negative numeric values are enclosed within parentheses

Not all flags apply to all format specifiers. The following sections explain each flag in detail.

Justifying Output

By default, all output is right-justified. That is, if the field width is larger than the data printed, the data will be placed on the right edge of the field. You can force output to be left-justified by placing a minus sign directly after the %. For example, **%–10.2f** left-justifies a floating-point number with two decimal places in a ten-character field. For example, consider this program:

```
// Demonstrate left justification.
import java.util.*;

class LeftJustify {
  public static void main(String args[]) {
    Formatter fmt = new Formatter();

    // Right justify by default.
    fmt.format("|%10.2f|", 123.123);
    System.out.println(fmt);

    // Now, left justify.
    fmt = new Formatter();
    fmt.format("|%-10.2f|", 123.123);
    System.out.println(fmt);
  }
}
```

It produces the following output:

```
|    123.12|
|123.12    |
```

As you can see, the second line is left-justified within a ten-character field.

The Space, +, 0, and (Flags

To cause a + sign to be shown before positive numeric values, add the + flag. For example,

```
fmt.format("%+d", 100);
```

creates this string:

```
+100
```

When creating columns of numbers it is sometimes useful to output a space before positive values so that positive and negative values line up. To do this, add the space flag. For example:

```
// Demonstrate the space format specifiers.
import java.util.*;

class FormatDemo5 {
  public static void main(String args[]) {
    Formatter fmt = new Formatter();

    fmt.format("% d", -100);
    System.out.println(fmt);

    fmt = new Formatter();
    fmt.format("% d", 100);
    System.out.println(fmt);

    fmt = new Formatter();
    fmt.format("% d", -200);
    System.out.println(fmt);

    fmt = new Formatter();
    fmt.format("% d", 200);
    System.out.println(fmt);
  }
}
```

The output is shown here:

```
-100
 100
-200
 200
```

Notice that the positive values have a leading space, which causes the digits in the column to line up properly.

To show negative numeric output inside parentheses, rather than with a leading –, use the (flag. For example,

```
fmt.format("%(d", -100);
```

creates this string:

```
(100)
```

The 0 flag causes output to be padded with zeros rather than spaces. The 0 flag can be used with all format specifiers except **%n**.

The Comma Flag

When displaying large numbers it is often useful to add grouping separators, which, in English, are commas. For example, the value 1234567 is more easily read when formatted as 1,234,567. To add grouping specifiers, use the comma (,) flag. For example,

```
fmt.format("%,.2f", 4356783497.34);
```

creates this string:

```
4,356,783,497.34
```

The # Flag

The # flag can be applied to the **%o**, **%x**, **%e**, and **%f** format specifiers. For **%e** and **%f**, the # ensures that there will be a decimal point even if there are no decimal digits. If you precede the **%x** format specifier with a #, the hexadecimal number will be printed with a **0x** prefix. Preceding the **%o** specifier with # causes the number to be printed with a leading zero.

The Uppercase Option

As mentioned earlier, several of the format specifiers have uppercase versions that cause the conversion to use uppercase where appropriate. The following table describes the effect.

Specifier	Effect
%A	Causes the hexadecimal digits *a* through *f* to be displayed in uppercase as *A* through *F*. Also, the prefix **0x** is displayed as **0X**, and **p** is displayed as **P**.
%B	Uppercases the values true and false.
%C	Uppercases the corresponding character argument.

Specifier	Effect
%E	Causes the *e* symbol that indicates the exponent to be displayed in uppercase.
%G	Causes the *e* symbol that indicates the exponent to be displayed in uppercase.
%H	Causes the hexadecimal digits *a* through *f* to be displayed in uppercase as *A* through *F*.
%S	Uppercases the corresponding string.
%T	Causes all alphabetical output to be displayed in uppercase.
%X	Causes the hexadecimal digits *a* through *f* to be displayed in uppercase as *A* through *F*. Also, the optional prefix **0x** is displayed as **0X**, if present.

For example, this call

```
fmt.format("%X", 250);
```

creates this string:

```
FA
```

This call

```
fmt.format("%E", 123.1234);
```

creates this string:

```
1.231234E+02
```

Using an Argument Index

Formatter includes a very useful feature that lets you specify the argument to which a format specifier applies. Normally, format specifiers and arguments are matched in order, from left to right. That is, the first format specifier matches the first argument, the second format specifier matches the second argument, and so on. However, by using an *argument index* you can explicitly control which argument a format specifier matches.

An argument index immediately follows the % in a format specifier. It has the following format:

n$

where *n* is the index of the desired argument, beginning with 1. For example, consider this example:

```
fmt.format("%3$d %1$d %2$d", 10, 20, 30);
```

It produces this string:

```
30 10 20
```

In this example, the first format specifier matches 30, the second matches 10, and the third matches 20. Thus, the arguments are used in an order other than strictly left to right.

One advantage of argument indexes is that they enable you to reuse an argument without having to specify it twice. For example, consider this line:

```
fmt.format("%d in hex is %1$x", 255);
```

It produces the following string:

```
255 in hex is ff
```

As you can see, the argument 255 is used by both format specifiers.

There is a convenient shorthand called a *relative index* that enables you to reuse the argument matched by the preceding format specifier. Simply specify < for the argument index. For example, the following call to **format( )** produces the same results as the previous example:

```
fmt.format("%d in hex is %<x", 255);
```

Relative indexes are especially useful when creating custom time and date formats. Consider the following example:

```
// Use relative indexes to simplify the
// creation of a custom time and date format.
import java.util.*;

class FormatDemo6 {
  public static void main(String args[]) {
    Formatter fmt = new Formatter();
    Calendar cal = Calendar.getInstance();
```

```
    fmt.format("Today is day %te of %<tB, %<tY", cal);
    System.out.println(fmt);
  }
}
```

Here is sample output:

```
Today is day 8 of May, 2004
```

Because of relative indexing, the argument **cal** need only be passed once, rather than three times.

Using Java's printf( ) Method

Although there is nothing technically wrong with using **Formatter** directly, as the preceding examples have done, when creating output that will be displayed on the console, Java 2, v5.0 offers a more convenient alternative: the **printf( )** method. The **printf( )** method automatically uses **Formatter** to create a formatted string. It then displays that string on standard out, which is the console by default. The **printf( )** method is defined by both **PrintStream** and **PrintWriter**.

For **PrintStream**, **printf( )** has these forms:

PrintStream printf(String *fmtString*, Object ... *args*)

PrintStream printf(Local *loc*, String *fmtString*, Object ... *args*)

The first version writes *args* to standard output in the format specified by *fmtString*, using the default locale. The second lets you specify a locale. Both return the invoking **PrintStream**. Because **System.out** is a **PrintStream**, you can call **printf( )** on **System.out**, directly.

The versions of **printf( )** for **PrintWriter** are shown next:

PrintWriter printf(String *fmtString*, Object ... *args*)

PrintWriter printf(Local *loc*, String *fmtString*, Object ... *args*)

These work just like the ones in **PrintStream** except that the invoking **PrintWriter** is returned.

Here is an example that uses **printf( )** to output numeric values in various formats. In the past, such formatting required a bit of work. With the addition of **printf( )**, this now becomes an easy task.

```
// Demonstrate printf().

class PrintfDemo {
  public static void main(String args[]) {
    System.out.println("Here are some numeric values " +
                       "in different formats.\n");

    System.out.printf("Various integer formats: ");
    System.out.printf("%d %(d %+d %05d\n", 3, -3, 3, 3);

    System.out.println();

    System.out.printf("Default floating-point format: %f\n",
                      1234567.123);
    System.out.printf("Floating-point with commas: %,f\n",
                      1234567.123);
    System.out.printf("Negative floating-point default: %,f\n",
                      -1234567.123);
    System.out.printf("Negative floating-point option: %,(f\n",
                      -1234567.123);

    System.out.println();

    System.out.printf("Line-up positive and negative values:\n");
    System.out.printf("% ,.2f\n% ,.2f\n",
                      1234567.123, -1234567.123);

  }
}
```

The output is shown here:

```
Here are some numeric values in different formats.

Various integer formats: 3 (3) +3 00003

Default floating-point format: 1234567.123000
Floating-point with commas: 1,234,567.123000
```

```
Negative floating-point default: -1,234,567.123000
Negative floating-point option: (1,234,567.123000)

Line-up positive and negative values:
 1,234,567.12
-1,234,567.12
```

Scanner

Scanner is the complement of **Formatter**. **Scanner** reads formatted input and
converts it into its binary form. It can be used to read input from the console, a
file, a string, or any source that implements the **Readable** interface (added by
Java 2, v5.0) or **ReadableByteChannel**. For example, you can use **Scanner** to
read a number from the keyboard and assign its value to a variable. Although
such operations have always been possible, **Scanner** greatly simplifies this
process. As you will see, given its power, **Scanner** is surprisingly easy to use.
    Scanner is packaged in **java.util**.

The Scanner Constructors

Scanner defines the constructors shown in Table 9-4. In general, a **Scanner** can
be created for a **String**, an **InputStream**, or any object that implements the
Readable or **ReadableByteChannel** interfaces.
    The following sequence creates a **Scanner** that reads the file **Test.txt**:

```
FileReader fin = new FileReader("Test.txt");
Scanner src = new Scanner(fin);
```

This works because **FileReader** implements the **Readable** interface. Thus, the
call to the constructor resolves to **Scanner(Readable)**.
    This next line creates a **Scanner** that reads from standard input, which is the
keyboard by default:

```
Scanner conin = new Scanner(System.in);
```

This works because **System.in** is an object of type **InputStream**. Thus, the call
to the constructor maps to **Scanner(InputStream)**.

Method	Description
static Scanner create(File *from*) throws FileNotFoundException	Creates a **Scanner** that uses the file specified by *from* as a source for input.
static Scanner create(File *from*, String *charset*) throws FileNotFoundException	Creates a **Scanner** that uses the file specified by *from* with the encoding specified by *charset* as a source for input.
Scanner(InputStream *from*)	Creates a **Scanner** that uses the stream specified by *from* as a source for input.
Scanner(InputStream *from*, String *charset*)	Creates a **Scanner** that uses the stream specified by *from* with the encoding specified by *charset* as a source for input.
Scanner(Readable *from*)	Creates a **Scanner** that uses the **Readable** object specified by *from* as a source for input.
Scanner(ReadableByteChannel *from*)	Creates a **Scanner** that uses the **ReadableByteChannel** specified by *from* as a source for input.
Scanner(ReadableByteChannel *from*, String *charset*)	Creates a **Scanner** that uses the **ReadableByteChannel** specified by *from* with the encoding specified by *charset* as a source for input.
Scanner(String *from*)	Creates a **Scanner** that uses the string specified by *from* as a source for input.

Table 9-4   *The **Scanner** Constructors*

The next sequence creates a **Scanner** that reads from a string:

```
String instr = "10 99.88 scanning is easy.";
Scanner conin = new Scanner(instr);
```

Scanning Basics

Once you have created a **Scanner**, it is a simple matter to use it to read formatted input. In general, a **Scanner** reads *tokens* from the underlying source that you specified when the **Scanner** was created. As it relates to **Scanner**, a token is a portion of input that is delineated by a set of delimiters, which is whitespace by default. A token is read by matching it with a particular *regular expression,* which defines the format of the data. Although **Scanner** allows you to define the specific type of expression that its next input operation will match, it includes many predefined patterns, which match the primitive types, such as **int** and **double**, and strings. Thus, often you won't need to specify a pattern to match.

In general, to use **Scanner**, follow this procedure:

1. Determine if a specific type of input is available by calling one of **Scanner**'s **hasNext**X methods, where X is the type of data desired.

2. If input is available, read it by calling one of **Scanner**'s **next**X methods.

3. Repeat the process until input is exhausted.

As the preceding indicates, **Scanner** defines two sets of methods that enable you to read input. The first are the **hasNext**X methods, which are shown in Table 9-5. These methods determine if the specified type of input is available. For example, calling **hasNextInt( )** returns true only if the next token to be read is an integer. If the desired data is available, then you read it by calling one of **Scanner**'s **next**X methods, which are shown in Table 9-6. For example, to read the next integer, call **nextInt( )**. The following sequence shows how to read a list of integers from the keyboard:

```
Scanner conin = new Scanner(System.in);
int i;

// Read a list of integers.
while(conin.hasNextInt()) {
  i = conin.nextInt();
  // ...
}
```

Method	Description
boolean hasNext( )	Returns true if another token of any type is available to be read. Returns false otherwise.
boolean hasNext(Pattern *pattern*)	Returns true if a token that matches the pattern passed in *pattern* is available to be read. Returns false otherwise.
boolean hasNext(String *pattern*)	Returns true if a token that matches the pattern passed in *pattern* is available to be read. Returns false otherwise.
boolean hasNextBigDecimal( )	Returns true if a value that can be stored in a **BigDecimal** object is available to be read. Returns false otherwise.
boolean hasNextBigInteger( )	Returns true if a value that can be stored in a **BigInteger** object is available to be read. Returns false otherwise. The default radix is used. (Unless changed, the default radix is 10.)
boolean hasNextBigInteger(int *radix*)	Returns true if a value in the specified radix that can be stored in a **BigInteger** object is available to be read. Returns false otherwise.

Table 9-5 *The Scanner hasNext Methods*

Method	Description
boolean hasNextBoolean( )	Returns true if a **boolean** value is available to be read. Returns false otherwise.
boolean hasNextByte( )	Returns true if a **byte** value is available to be read. Returns false otherwise. The default radix is used. (Unless changed, the default radix is 10.)
boolean hasNextByte(int *radix*)	Returns true if a **byte** value in the specified radix is available to be read. Returns false otherwise.
boolean hasNextDouble( )	Returns true if a **double** value is available to be read. Returns false otherwise.
boolean hasNextFloat( )	Returns true if a **float** value is available to be read. Returns false otherwise.
boolean hasNextInt( )	Returns true if an **int** value is available to be read. Returns false otherwise. The default radix is used. (Unless changed, the default radix is 10.)
boolean hasNextInt(int *radix*)	Returns true if an **int** value in the specified radix is available to be read. Returns false otherwise.
boolean hasNextLong( )	Returns true if a **long** value is available to be read. Returns false otherwise. The default radix is used. (Unless changed, the default radix is 10.)
boolean hasNextLong(int *radix*)	Returns true if a **long** value in the specified radix is available to be read. Returns false otherwise.
boolean hasNextShort( )	Returns true if a **short** value is available to be read. Returns false otherwise. The default radix is used. (Unless changed, the default radix is 10.)
boolean hasNextShort(int *radix*)	Returns true if a **short** value in the specified radix is available to be read. Returns false otherwise.

Table 9-5   *The **Scanner hasNext** Methods* (continued)

Method	Description
String next( )	Returns the next token of any type from the input source.
String next(Pattern *pattern*)	Returns the next token that matches the pattern passed in *pattern* from the input source.
String next(String *pattern*)	Returns the next token that matches the pattern passed in *pattern* from the input source.
BigDecimal nextBigDecimal( )	Returns the next token as a **BigDecimal** object.
BigInteger nextBigInteger( )	Returns the next token as a **BigInteger** object. The default radix is used. (Unless changed, the default radix is 10.)
BigInteger nextBigInteger(int *radix*)	Returns the next token (using the specified radix) as a **BigInteger** object.
boolean nextBoolean( )	Returns the next token as a **boolean** value.

Table 9-6   *The **Scanner next** Methods*

Method	Description
byte nextByte( )	Returns the next token as a **byte** value. The default radix is used. (Unless changed, the default radix is 10.)
byte nextByte(int *radix*)	Returns the next token (using the specified radix) as a **byte** value.
double nextDouble( )	Returns the next token as a **double** value.
float nextFloat( )	Returns the next token as a **float** value.
int nextInt( )	Returns the next token as an **int** value. The default radix is used. (Unless changed, the default radix is 10.)
int nextInt(int *radix*)	Returns the next token (using the specified radix) as an **int** value.
long nextLong( )	Returns the next token as a **long** value. The default radix is used. (Unless changed, the default radix is 10.)
long nextLong(int *radix*)	Returns the next token (using the specified radix) as a **long** value.
short nextShort( )	Returns the next token as a **short** value. The default radix is used. (Unless changed, the default radix is 10.)
short nextShort(int *radix*)	Returns the next token (using the specified radix) as a **short** value.

Table 9-6 *The Scanner next Methods* (continued)

The **while** loop stops as soon as the next token is not an integer. Thus, the loop stops reading integers as soon as a non-integer is encountered in the input stream.

If a **next** method cannot find the type of data it is looking for, it throws a **NoSuchElementException**. For this reason, it is best to first confirm that the desired type of data is available by calling a **hasNext** method before calling its corresponding **next** method.

Some Scanner Examples

The addition of **Scanner** to Java makes what was formerly a tedious task into an easy one. To understand why, let's look at some examples. The following program averages a list of numbers entered at the keyboard:

```
// Use Scanner to compute an average of the values.
import java.util.*;

class AvgNums {
  public static void main(String args[]) {
    Scanner conin = new Scanner(System.in);

    int count = 0;
    double sum = 0.0;
```

```
System.out.println("Enter numbers to average.");

// Read and sum numbers.
while(conin.hasNext()) {
  if(conin.hasNextDouble()) {
    sum += conin.nextDouble();
    count++;
  }
  else {
    String str = conin.next();
    if(str.equals("done")) break;
    else {
      System.out.println("Data format error.");
      return;
    }
  }
}

System.out.println("Average is " + sum / count);
  }
}
```

The program reads numbers from the keyboard, summing them in the process, until the user enters the string "done". It then stops input and displays the average of the numbers. Here is a sample run:

```
Enter numbers to average.
1.2
2
3.4
4
done
Average is 2.65
```

The program reads numbers until it encounters a token that does not represent a valid **double** value. When this occurs, it confirms that the token is the string "done". If it is, the program terminates normally. Otherwise, it displays an error.

Notice that the numbers are read by calling **nextDouble( )**. This method reads any number that can be converted into a **double** value, including an integer value, such as 2, and a floating-point value like 3.4. Thus, a number read by **nextDouble( )** need not specify a decimal point. This same general principle applies to all **next** methods. They will match and read any data format that can represent the type of value being requested.

One thing that is especially nice about **Scanner** is that the same technique used to read from one source can be used to read from another. For example, here is the preceding program reworked to average a list of numbers contained in a text file:

```java
// Use Scanner to compute an average of the values in a file.
import java.util.*;
import java.io.*;

class AvgFile {
  public static void main(String args[])
    throws IOException {

    int count = 0;
    double sum = 0.0;

    // Write output to a file.
    FileWriter fout = new FileWriter("test.txt");
    fout.write("2 3.4 5 6 7.4 9.1 10.5 done");
    fout.close();

    FileReader fin = new FileReader("Test.txt");

    Scanner src = new Scanner(fin);

    // Read and sum numbers.
    while(src.hasNext()) {
      if(src.hasNextDouble()) {
        sum += src.nextDouble();
        count++;
      }
      else {
        String str = src.next();
        if(str.equals("done")) break;
        else {
          System.out.println("File format error.");
          return;
        }
      }
    }

    fin.close();
    System.out.println("Average is " + sum / count);
  }
}
```

```
Average is 6.2
```

You can use **Scanner** to read input that contains several different types of data—even if the order of that data is unknown in advance. You must simply check what type of data is available before reading it. For example, consider this program:

```java
// Use Scanner to read various types of data from a file.
import java.util.*;
import java.io.*;

class ScanMixed {
  public static void main(String args[])
    throws IOException {

    int i;
    double d;
    boolean b;
    String str;

    // Write output to a file.
    FileWriter fout = new FileWriter("test.txt");
    fout.write("Testing Scanner 10 12.2 one true two false");
    fout.close();

    FileReader fin = new FileReader("Test.txt");

    Scanner src = new Scanner(fin);


    // Read to end.
    while(src.hasNext()) {
      if(src.hasNextInt()) {
        i = src.nextInt();
        System.out.println("int: " + i);
      }
      else if(src.hasNextDouble()) {
        d = src.nextDouble();
        System.out.println("double: " + d);
      }
      else if(src.hasNextBoolean()) {
        b = src.nextBoolean();
        System.out.println("boolean: " + b);
      }
```

```
      else {
        str = src.next();
        System.out.println("String: " + str);
      }
    }
  }

    fin.close();
  }
}
```

Here is the output:

```
String: Testing
String: Scanner
int: 10
double: 12.2
String: one
boolean: true
String: two
boolean: false
```

When reading mixed data types, as the preceding program does, you need to be a bit careful about the order in which you call the **next** methods. For example, if the loop reversed the order of the calls to **nextInt( )** and **nextDouble( )**, both numeric values would have been read as **double**s, because **nextDouble( )** matches any numeric string that can be represented as a **double**.

Setting Delimiters

Scanner defines where a token starts and ends based on a set of *delimiters*. The default delimiters are the whitespace characters, and this is the delimiter set that the preceding examples have used. However, it is possible to change the delimiters by calling the **useDelimiter( )** method, shown here:

> Scanner useDelimiter(String *pattern*)

> Scanner useDelimiter(Pattern *pattern*)

Here, *pattern* is a regular expression that specifies the delimiter set.

Here is a program that reworks the average program shown earlier so that it reads a list of numbers that are separated by commas, and any number of spaces:

```java
// Use Scanner to compute the average of a list of
// comma-separated values.
import java.util.*;
import java.io.*;

class SetDelimiters {
  public static void main(String args[])
    throws IOException {

    int count = 0;
    double sum = 0.0;

    // Write output to a file.
    FileWriter fout = new FileWriter("test.txt");

    // Now, store values in comma-separated list.
    fout.write("2, 3.4,    5,6, 7.4, 9.1, 10.5, done");
    fout.close();

    FileReader fin = new FileReader("Test.txt");

    Scanner src = new Scanner(fin);

    // Set delimiters to space and comma.
    src.useDelimiter(", *");

    // Read and sum numbers.
    while(src.hasNext()) {
      if(src.hasNextDouble()) {
        sum += src.nextDouble();
        count++;
      }
      else {
        String str = src.next();
        if(str.equals("done")) break;
        else {
          System.out.println("File format error.");
          return;
        }
      }
    }

    fin.close();
    System.out.println("Average is " + sum / count);
  }
}
```

In this version, the numbers written to **test.txt** are separated by commas and spaces. The use of the delimiter pattern ", *" tells **Scanner** to match a comma and zero or more spaces as delimiters. The output is the same as before.

You can obtain the current delimiter pattern by calling **delimiter( )**, shown here:

> Pattern delimiter( )

Other Scanner Features

Scanner defines several other methods in addition to those already discussed. One that is particularly useful in some circumstances is **findInLine( )**. Its general forms are shown here:

> String findInLine(Pattern *pattern*)

> String findInLine(String *pattern*)

This method searches for the specified pattern within the next line of text. If the pattern is found, the matching token is consumed and returned. Otherwise, null is returned. It operates independently of any delimiter set. This method is useful if you want to locate a specific pattern. For example, the following program locates the Age field in the input string and then displays the age:

```
// Demonstrate findInLine().
import java.util.*;

class FindInLineDemo {
  public static void main(String args[]) {
    String instr = "Name: Tom Age: 28 ID: 77";

    Scanner conin = new Scanner(instr);

    // Find and display age.
    conin.findInLine("Age:"); // find Age

    if(conin.hasNext())
      System.out.println(conin.next());
    else
      System.out.println("Error!");

  }
}
```

The output is **28**. In the program, **findInLine( )** is used to find an occurrence of the pattern "Age". Once found, the next token is read, which is the age.

Related to **findInLine( )** is **findWithinHorizon( )**, shown here:

String findWithinHorizon(Pattern *pattern*, int *count*)

String findWithinHorizon (String *pattern*, int *count*)

This method attempts to find an occurrence of the specified pattern within the next *count* characters. If successful, it returns the matching pattern. Otherwise, it returns null. If *count* is zero, then all input is searched until either a match is found or the end of input is encountered.

You can bypass a pattern using **skip( )**, shown here:

Scanner skip(Pattern *pattern*)

Scanner skip(String *pattern*)

If *pattern* is matched, **skip( )** simply advances beyond it and returns a reference to the invoking object. If pattern is not found, **skip( )** throws **NoSuchElementException**.

Other **Scanner** methods include **radix( )**, which returns the default radix used by the **Scanner**, **useRadix( )**, which sets the radix, and **close( )**, which closes the scanner.

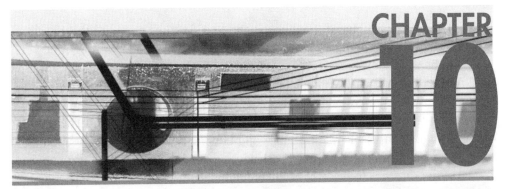

CHAPTER 10

Changes to the API

The primary focus of this book is the new features added to the Java language, and those features were described by the preceding nine chapters. However, Java 2, v5.0 also caused many changes to the Java API. As has been the case with all Java revisions, many of the changes to the API are small, involving incremental improvements or tweaks to the existing library. However, a few are quite significant and affect all Java programmers. These changes involve either the addition of major new features or significant updates to existing features. It is these major changes that are the subject of this chapter.

The major changes to the API are listed here:

- The retrofitting of the Collections Framework (and other portions of the API) for generics
- New classes and interfaces added to **java.lang**
- Bit-manipulation methods added to **Integer** and **Long**
- Support for 32-bit Unicode code points in the **String** and **Character** classes
- Several new subpackages added to **java.lang**
- Several new subpackages added to **java.util**

Because of the care that was taken by the Java design team, these extensive additions and updates were accomplished without breaking existing code, and substantial power has been added to the API. The remainder of this chapter offers an overview of these changes.

Collections Are Retrofitted for Generics

The most significant change to the API is found in the classes, interfaces, and methods that form the Collections Framework. Each was completely overhauled and upgraded to operate on a parameterized type, rather than on references of type **Object**. Making the Collections Framework generic is a major advance because operations on collections are now type-safe. Generics also eliminate the need to cast an element contained in a collection back into its proper type when that element is retrieved.

In general, all of the collection classes and interfaces have been given type parameters that describe the type of the element stored or manipulated by the collection. Here is how the collection interfaces are now declared:

interface Collection<E>

interface Iterator<E>

interface List<E>

interface Queue<E>

interface SortedMap<K, V>

interface Comparator<T>

interface ListIterator<E>

interface Map<K, V>

interface Set<E>

interface SortedSet<E>

In the above list, the class **Queue** was added by Java 2, v5.0.

Here is how the collection classes are now declared:

abstract class AbstractCollection<E>

abstract class AbstractMap<K, V>

abstract class AbstractSequentialList<E>

class ArrayList<E>

class EnumMap<K extends Enum<K>, V>

class HashMap<K, V>

class HashTable<K, V>

class LinkedHashMap<K, V>

class LinkedList<E>

class Stack<E>

class TreeSet<E>

class WeakHashMap<K, V>

abstract class AbstractList<E>

abstract class AbstractQueue<E>

abstract class AbstractSet<E>

class Collections

class EnumSet<E extends Enum<E>>

class HashSet<E>

class IdentifyHashMap<K, V>

class LinkedHashSet<E>

class PriorityQueue<E>

class TreeMap<K, V>

class Vector<E>

In the above list, the classes **EnumMap**, **EnumSet**, **AbstractQueue**, and **PriorityQueue** were added by Java 2, v5.0.

Now that the Collections Framework is generic, when you create a collection, you specify the type of data that the collection will hold. For example,

```
ArrayList<Integer> list = new ArrayList<Integer>();
```

declares **list** as a reference to an **ArrayList** that holds **Integer** objects.

Because **Iterator** is also generic, you must specify the type of data that the iterator will be retrieving as a type parameter. For example, assuming **list** is declared as just shown, this obtains an iterator that is compatible with it:

```
Iterator<Integer> itr = list.iterator();
```

Because **list** holds **Integer**s, **itr** must be declared as being an iterator for objects of type **Integer**.

Updates to the Collections Class

Notice in the above list of collection classes that **Collections** does *not* take a generic type parameter. This is because the **Collections** class is comprised exclusively of static methods that implement algorithms that manipulate collections. Thus, there is no reason for **Collections** to be generic. However, its methods *are* updated for generics, by using generic parameters or by having generic return types.

Several new methods have also been added to **Collections**. Perhaps the most important is the set of overloaded **checked** methods, such as **checkedCollection( )**, which returns what the API documentation refers to as a "runtime type-safe view" of a collection. This view is a reference to the collection that monitors insertions into the collection for type compatibility, dynamically, at run time. An attempt to insert an incompatible element will cause a **ClassCastException**. Using such a view is helpful during debugging because it ensures that the collection always contains valid elements. Related methods include **checkedSet( )**, **checkedList( )**, **checkedMap( )**, and so on. They obtain a type-safe view for the indicated collection.

Other new methods are

- **frequency( )**, which returns the number of occurrences of an element.
- **disjoint( )**, which returns true if two collections share no common elements.
- **addAll( )**, which adds the contents of an array to a collection.
- **reverseOrder( )**, which returns a reverse-order **Comparator**.

Why Generic Collections?

A detailed discussion of the advantages of generics as they apply to collections is found in Chapter 3. However, a brief summary is presented here.

In the past, a collection stored only **Object** references, which could refer to any type of object. Now, you specify explicitly what type of data is stored in the collection. For example,

```
LinkedList<String> list = new LinkedList<String>();
```

declares **list** to be a **LinkedList** that stores objects of type **String**.

Because **list** is declared as storing **String** references, these are the only kind of references that can be added to it. For example, the statement

```
list.add("Collections");
```

is valid because a quoted string is a **String**. However, this next statement is invalid because it attempts to store an **Integer** in **list**:

```
list.add(new Integer(10)); // Error!
```

This will cause a type-mismatch error because **Integer** is incompatible with **String**.

Another advantage of adding generic support to collections is that it is no longer necessary to apply a type cast when retrieving objects from a collection. For example, in old-style code, to retrieve a string from **list**, you would write a statement like this:

```
String str = (String) list.get(0); // old-style code
```

In the past, the type cast was needed because the return type of **list.get( )** was **Object**, not **String**. With the addition of generics, you now write the statement like this:

```
String str = list.get(0); // new-style, type String is automatic
```

Because **list** is of type **LinkedList<String>**, the compiler automatically knows that the reference returned by **list.get( )** is a **String** and no explicit cast is needed.

Aside from convenience, the elimination of explicit casts also prevents errors. It is not possible to accidentally cast the reference returned by a method such as **get( )** into an incompatible type. In the past, such incorrect casts resulted in run-time errors. With generics, incorrect casts are caught at compile time, where they can be fixed before code is put into use.

Other Classes and Interfaces Retrofitted for Generics

Several other classes, interfaces, and methods in Java's API have been retrofitted for generics. For example, in **java.lang** the following interfaces and classes are now generic:

Comparable<T>   Class<T>   ThreadLocal<T>

The new **Enum** class and **Iterable** interface are also generic. In **java.lang.reflect**, **Constructor** is now generic.

Furthermore, many preexisting methods now take generic parameters. For example, the **getClass( )** method, which is a member of **Object**, now returns a generic reference of type **Class<T extends Object>**. Another example is the **getenv( )** method in **System**. Java 2, v5.0 added an overloaded form that returns a generic **Map**. Also, the classes **Constructor**, **Method**, **Field**, **Package**, and **Class** all have been upgraded to support annotations. One of the annotation methods is **getAnnotation( )**, which returns a generic type.

New Classes and Interfaces Added to java.lang

Java 2, v5.0 adds three new classes and three new interfaces to **java.lang**.
The new classes are

Enum   ProcessBuilder   StringBuilder

The new interfaces are

Appendable   Iterable<T>   Readable

Enum is described in detail in Chapter 6. The remaining classes and interfaces are described here.

The ProcessBuilder Class

ProcessBuilder is a new class added to **java.lang**. It provides a way to start and manage processes (that is, programs). As you may recall, all processes are represented by the **Process** class, and prior to Java 2, v5.0, a process was started by calling **Runtime.exec( )**. **ProcessBuilder** offers more control over processes than was previously available. For example, you can set the current working directory and change environmental parameters.

ProcessBuilder defines these constructors:

ProcessBuilder(List<String> *args*)

ProccessBuilder(String ... *args*)

Here, *args* is a list of arguments that specifies the name of the program to execute along with any required command-line arguments. In the first constructor, the arguments are passed in a **List**. In the second, they are specified through a varargs parameter. Table 10-1 describes the methods defined by **ProcessBuilder**.

Method	Description
List<String> command( )	Returns a reference to a **List** that contains the name of the program and its arguments. Changes to this list affect the invoking process.
ProcessBuilder command(List<String> *args*)	Sets the name of the program and its arguments to those specified by *args*. Changes to this list affect the invoking process.
ProcessBuilder command(String ... *args*)	Sets the name of the program and its arguments to those specified by *args*.
File directory( )	Returns the current working directory of the invoking **ProcessBuilder**. This value will be null if the directory is the same as that of the Java program that started the process.
ProcessBuilder directory(File *dir*)	Sets the current working directory of the invoking **ProcessBuilder**.

Table 10-1   *The Methods Defined by **ProcessBuilder***

Method	Description
Map<String, String> environment( )	Returns the environmental variables associated with the invoking **ProcessBuilder** as key/value pairs.
boolean redirectErrorStream( )	Returns true if the standard error stream has been redirected to the standard output stream. Returns false if the streams are separate.
ProcessBuilder redirectErrorStream(boolean *merge*)	If *merge* is true, then the standard error steam is redirected to standard output. If *merge* is false, the streams are separated, which is the default state.
Process start( ) throws IOException	Begins the process specified by the invoking **ProcessBuilder**.

Table 10-1   *The Methods Defined by **ProcessBuilder*** (continued)

To create a process using **ProcessBuilder**, you simply create an instance of **ProcessBuilder**, specifying the name of the program and any needed arguments. To begin execution of the program, call **start( )** on that instance. Here is a simple example that executes the Windows text editor Notepad. Notice that it specifies the name of the file to edit as an argument.

```
// Demonstrate ProcessBuilder.
import java.io.*;

class PBDemo {
  public static void main(String args[])
    throws IOException {

    ProcessBuilder proc = new ProcessBuilder("notepad.exe", "testfile");
    proc.start();
  }
}
```

The StringBuilder Class

StringBuilder is identical to Java's well-known **StringBuffer** class except for one important difference: it is not synchronized, which means that it is not thread-safe.

The advantage of using **StringBuilder** is faster performance. However, in cases in which you are using multithreading, you must use **StringBuffer** rather than **StringBuilder**.

The **String** class defines a new constructor that enables you to construct a **String** from a **StringBuilder**. It is shown here:

String(StringBuilder *strBuildObj*)

The Appendable Interface

An object of a class that implements **Appendable** can have characters or character sequences appended to it. **Appendable** defines these two methods:

Appendable append(char *ch*) throws IOException

Appendable append(CharSequence *chars*) throws IOException

In the first form, the character *ch* is appended to the invoking object. In the second form, the character sequence *chars* is appended to the invoking object. In both cases, a reference to the invoking object is returned.

The Iterable Interface

The interface **Iterable** must be implemented by any class whose objects will be used by the for-each version of the **for** loop. In other words, in order for an object to be used within a for-each style **for** loop, its class must implement **Iterable**. **Iterable** is a generic interface that has this declaration:

interface Iterable<T>

It defines one method, **iterator( )**, which is shown here:

Iterator<T> iterator( )

It returns an iterator to the set of elements contained in the invoking object.

The Readable Interface

The **Readable** interface indicates that an object can be used as a source for characters. It defines one method, called **read( )**, which is shown here:

    int read(CharBuffer *cb*) throws IOException

This method reads characters into *cb*. It returns the number of characters read, or −1 if an EOF is encountered.

Bit-Manipulation Methods Added to Integer and Long

Several bit-manipulation methods were added to the numeric type wrappers **Integer** and **Long**. The bit-manipulation methods added to **Integer** are shown in Table 10-2. **Long** has similar methods except that they operate on data of type **long**. They are shown in Table 10-3.

Method	Description
static int bitCount(int *num*)	Returns the number of one bits in *num*.
static int highestOneBit(int *num*)	Determines the position of the highest order one bit in *num*. It returns a value in which only this bit is set. If no bit is set to one, then zero is returned.
static int lowestOneBit(int *num*)	Determines the position of the lowest order one bit in *num*. It returns a value in which only this bit is set. If no bit is set to one, then zero is returned.
static int numberOfLeadingZeros(int *num*)	Returns the number of high-order zero bits that precede the first high-order one bit in *num*. 32 is returned if *num* is zero.
static int numberOfTrailingZeros(int *num*)	Returns the number of high-order zero bits that follow the first low-order one bit in *num*. 32 is returned if *num* is zero.
static int reverse(int *num*)	Reverses the order of the bits in *num* and returns the result.
static int rotateLeft(int *num*, int *n*)	Returns the result of rotating *num* left *n* positions.
static int rotateRight(int *num*, int *n*)	Returns the result of rotating *num* right *n* positions.

Table 10-2   *The Bit-Manipulation Methods Added to **Integer***

Method	Description
static int bitCount(long *num*)	Returns the number of one bits in *num*.
static long highestOneBit(long *num*)	Determines the position of the highest order one bit in *num*. It returns a value in which only this bit is set. If no bit is set to one, then zero is returned.
static long lowestOneBit(long *num*)	Determines the position of the lowest order one bit in *num*. It returns a value in which only this bit is set. If no bit is set to one, then zero is returned.
static int numberOfLeadingZeros(long *num*)	Returns the number of high-order zero bits that precede the first high-order one bit in *num*. 64 is returned if *num* is zero.
static int numberOfTrailingZeros(long *num*)	Returns the number of high-order zero bits that follow the first low-order one bit in *num*. 64 is returned if *num* is zero.
static long reverse(long *num*)	Reverses the order of the bits in *num* and returns the result.
static long rotateLeft(long *num*, int *n*)	Returns the result of rotating *num* left *n* positions.
static long rotateRight(long *num*, int *n*)	Returns the result of rotating *num* right *n* positions.

Table 10-3   *The Bit-Manipulation Methods Added to **Long***

Here is a program that demonstrates some of the bit manipulations:

```
// Demonstrate several of the new bit manipulation
// methods in Integer.

class Bits {
  public static void main(String args[]) {
    int n = 170; // 10101010

    System.out.println("Value in binary: 10101010");

    System.out.println("Number of one bits: " +
                   Integer.bitCount(n));

    System.out.println("Highest one bit: " +
                   Integer.highestOneBit(n));

    System.out.println("Lowest one bit: " +
                   Integer.lowestOneBit(n));
```

```
System.out.println("Number of leading zeros : " +
                   Integer.numberOfLeadingZeros(n));

System.out.println("Number of trailing zeros : " +
                   Integer.numberOfTrailingZeros(n));

System.out.println("\nBeginning with the value 1, " +
                   "rotate left 16 times.");
n = 1;
for(int i=0; i < 16; i++) {
  n = Integer.rotateLeft(n, 1);
  System.out.println(n);
}
}
}
```

The output is shown here:

```
Value in binary: 10101010
Number of one bits: 4
Highest one bit: 128
Lowest one bit: 2
Number of leading zeros : 24
Number of trailing zeros : 1

Beginning with the value 1, rotate left 16 times.
2
4
8
16
32
64
128
256
512
1024
2048
4096
8192
16384
32768
65536
```

The signum( ) and reverseBytes( ) Methods

The numeric type wrappers **Integer** and **Long** added the methods **signum( )** and **reverseBytes( )**. The **Integer** versions of these methods are shown here:

static int signum(int *num*)

static int reverseBytes(int *num*)

signum( ) returns −1 if *num* is negative, 0 if it is zero, and 1 if it is positive. **reverseBytes( )** reverses the order of the bytes in *num* and returns the result.
    The **Long** versions of these methods are shown here:

static int signum(long *num*)

static long reverseBytes(long *num*)

They work the same as their **Integer** relatives.
    The **reverseBytes( )** method has also been added to **Short**.

Support for 32-Bit Unicode Code Points

Java 2, v5.0 made major additions to **Character** and **String** that provide support for 32-bit Unicode characters. In the past, all Unicode characters could be held by 16 bits, which is the size of a **char** (and the size of the value contained in a **Character**), because those values ranged from 0 to FFFF. However, recently, the Unicode character set has been expanded and requires more than 16 bits. This new version of Unicode has characters that range from 0 to 10FFFF.
    Here are three important terms: *code point, code unit,* and *supplemental character.* As it relates to Java, a code point is a character in the range 0 to 10FFFF. Java uses the term code unit to refer to the 16-bit characters. Characters that have values greater than FFFF are called supplemental characters.
    The expansion of the Unicode character set caused a fundamental problem for Java. Because a supplemental character has a value greater than a **char** can hold, some means of handling the supplemental characters was needed. Java 2, v5.0 addresses this problem two ways. First, Java uses two **char**s to represent a

supplemental character. The first **char** is called the *high surrogate* and the second is called the *low surrogate*. New methods, such as **codePointAt( )**, are provided that translate between code points and supplemental characters.

Secondly, Java overloaded several preexisting methods in the **Character** and **String** classes. The overloaded forms use **int** rather than **char** data. Because an **int** is large enough to hold any character as a single value, it can be used to store any character. For example, the method **isDigit( )** now has these two forms:

static boolean isDigit(char ch)

static boolean isDigit(int cp)

The first is the original version, the second is the version that supports 32-bit code points. All of the **is...** methods, such as **isLetter( )** and **isSpaceChar( )**, have code point forms, as do **to...** methods, such as **toUpperCase( )** and **toLowerCase( )**.

In addition to the methods overloaded to accept code points, Java 2, v5.0 has included new methods in **Character** that provide additional support for code points. A sampling is shown in Table 10-4.

Method	Description
static int charCount(int *cp*)	Returns 1 if *cp* can be represented by a single **char**. Returns 2 if two **char**s are needed.
static int codePointAt(CharSequence *chars*, int *loc*)	Returns the code point at the location specified by *loc*.
static int codePointAt(char *chars*[ ], int *loc*)	Returns the code point at the location specified by *loc*.
static int codePointBefore(CharSequence *chars*, int *loc*)	Returns the code point at the location that precedes that specified by *loc*.
static int codePointBefore(char *chars*[ ], int *loc*)	Returns the code point at the location that precedes that specified by *loc*.
static boolean isSupplementaryCodePoint(int *cp*)	Returns true if *cp* contains a supplemental character.
static boolean isHighSurrogate(char *ch*)	Returns true if *ch* contains a valid high surrogate character.
static boolean isLowSurrogate(char *ch*)	Returns true if *ch* contains a valid low surrogate character.

Table 10-4 *A Sampling of the **Character** Methods that Provide Support for 32-Bit Unicode Code Points*

Method	Description
static boolean isSurrogatePair(char *highCh*, char *lowCh*)	Returns true if *highCh* and *lowCh* form a valid surrogate pair.
static boolean isValidCodePoint(int *cp*)	Returns true if *cp* contains a valid code point.
static char[ ] toChars(int *cp*)	Converts the code point in *cp* into its **char** equivalent, which might require two **char**s. An array holding the result is returned.
static int toChars(int *cp*, char *target*[ ], int *loc*)	Converts the code point in *cp* into its **char** equivalent, storing the result in *target*, beginning at *loc*. Returns 1 if *cp* can be represented by a single **char**. It returns 2 otherwise.
static int toCodePoint(char *highCh*, char *lowCh*)	Converts *highCh* and *lowCh* into their equivalent code points.

Table 10-4   *A Sampling of the **Character** Methods that Provide Support for 32-Bit Unicode Code Points* (continued)

To support code points, the **String** class has the methods shown in Table 10-5. **String** also adds the following constructor that supports the extended Unicode character set:

String(int[] *codePoints*, int *startIndex*, int *numChars*)

Here, *codePoints* is an array that contains code points. The resulting string is constructed from the range that begins at *startIndex* and runs for *numChars* characters.

Method	Description
int codePointAt(int *i*)	Returns the code point at the location specified by *i*.
int codePointBefore(int *i*)	Returns the code point at the location that precedes that specified by *i*.
int codePointCount(int *start*, int *end*)	Returns the number of code points in the portion of the invoking **String** that is between *start* and *end*–1.
int offsetByCodePoints(int *start*, int *num*)	Returns the index within the invoking string that is *num* code points beyond the starting index specified by *start*.

Table 10-5   *The **String** Methods that Provide Support for 32-Bit Unicode Code Points*

New java.lang Subpackages

Java 2, v5.0 added the following subpackages to **java.lang**:

- **java.lang.annotation**
- **java.lang.instrument**
- **java.lang.management**

Each is briefly described here.

java.lang.annotation

Java's new annotation facility is supported by **java.lang.annotation**. It defines the **Annotation** interface, and the **ElementType** and **RetentionPolicy** enumerations. (Annotations are described in detail in Chapter 7.)

java.lang.instrument

java.lang.instrument defines features that can be used to add instrumentation to various aspects of program execution. It defines the **Instrumentation** and **ClassFileTransformer** interfaces, and the **ClassDefinition** class.

java.lang.management

The **java.lang.management** package provides management support for the JVM and the execution environment. Using the features in **java.lang.management**, you can observe and manage various aspects of program execution.

New java.util Subpackages

Java 2, v5.0 added the following subpackages to **java.util**:

- **java.util.concurrent**
- **java.util.concurrent.atomic**
- **java.util.concurrent.locks**

Each is briefly examined here.

java.util.concurrent

The **java.util.concurrent** package supports concurrent programming. This means that the classes defined in **java.util.concurrent** are thread-safe. Also added are two subpackages, **java.util.concurrent.atomic** and **java.util.concurrent.locks**. Collectively, these packages provide a high-performance alternative to using Java's built-in synchronization features when thread-safe operation is required. A principal advantage is that concurrent read (get) operations are supported, thus increasing speed.

    java.util.concurrent defines several concurrent collection classes, including **ConcurrentHashMap**, **ConcurrentLinkedQueue**, and **CopyOnWriteArraylist**, which offer concurrent alternatives to their related classes defined by the Collections Framework. Also defined is the **Semaphore** class. A semaphore gives you more control over how threads gain access to objects than does the **synchronized** keyword.

    Although they are a powerful addition to Java, the concurrent features added by **java.util.concurrent** and its subpackages are not for all programs. Rather, they are intended for highly concurrent environments or specialized applications. For most multithreaded situations, Java's built-in synchronization features are a better choice. Remember, Java's built-in support of synchronization is one of its key design features. It should not be abandoned lightly.

java.util.concurrent.atomic

java.util.concurrent.atomic facilitates the use of variables in a concurrent environment. It provides a means of efficiently updating the value of a variable without the use of locks. This is accomplished through the use of methods such as **compareAndSet( )**, **decrementAndGet( )**, and **getAndSet( )**.

java.util.concurrent.locks

java.util.concurrent.locks provides an alternative to Java's built-in synchronization features. At the core of this alternative is the **Lock** interface, which defines the basic mechanism used to acquire and relinquish access to an object. The key methods are **lock( )**, **tryLock( )**, and **unlock( )**. The advantage of these methods is greater control over synchronization. Of course, Java's built-in mechanism is cleaner and easier to use.

Formatter and Scanner

Java 2, v5.0 substantially upgrades its formatted I/O facilities with the **Formatter** and **Scanner** classes, which were added to **java.util**. These are described in depth in Chapter 9.

Index

@ (annotation syntax), 116, 117
< >, 23, 24, 32, 47
= =, 103, 111
< (relative index), 159–160
% (format conversion specifier syntax), 145
... (variable-length argument syntax), 93, 94, 97
? (wildcard argument specifier), 36, 44, 61

A

AbstractQueue class, 177
addAll( ), 178
AnnotatedElement interface, 124, 127
    methods defined by, table of, 125
Annotation interface, 116, 124, 190
Annotation(s), 4, 116–117, 180
    applying, 117
    built-in, 130–132
    marker, 127–128
    member, default value for, 125–126
    obtaining all, 122–124
    restrictions on, 132
    retention policy for, specifying, 117–118
    single-member, 128
    using reflection to obtain, 118–124
annotationType( ), 116
API changes, 3, 6, 176–192
Appendable interface, 147, 180
ArrayList class declaration, 66
Arrays
    and the for-each version of for, 78–84
    and generics, 75–76
    and variable-length arguments, 92–94
Argument index, 158–160

Argument, type. *See* Type argument(s)
Argument, wildcard. *See* Wildcard argument(s)
Arguments, variable-length. *See* Vararg(s)
Autoboxing/unboxing, 2, 4, 8–17, 25, 26
    Boolean and Character values, 14, 15
    definition of, 10
    and error prevention, 15–16
    and expressions, 12–14
    fundamentals of, 10–11
    and methods, 11–12
    when to use, 16–17

B

Bit-manipulation methods, 184–186
Boolean object to control loop statements, using, 15
Boolean type wrapper class, 8, 14
Boxing (manual), 9
Bridge methods, 70–72
Byte type wrapper class, 8
byteValue( ), 9, 16

C

Calendar class, 148
Casts, 3, 21, 24, 25, 27, 28, 29, 176
    and casting one instance of a generic class into another, 61–62
    and erasure, 68–69
    and pre-generics collections, 65, 179
Character type wrapper class, 8
    support for 32-bit Unicode, 176, 187–189

INTERNATIONAL CONTACT INFORMATION

AUSTRALIA
McGraw-Hill Book Company
Australia Pty. Ltd.
TEL +61-2-9900-1800
FAX +61-2-9878-8881
http://www.mcgraw-hill.com.au
books-it_sydney@mcgraw-hill.com

CANADA
McGraw-Hill Ryerson Ltd.
TEL +905-430-5000
FAX +905-430-5020
http://www.mcgraw-hill.ca

GREECE, MIDDLE EAST, & AFRICA
(Excluding South Africa)
McGraw-Hill Hellas
TEL +30-210-6560-990
TEL +30-210-6560-993
TEL +30-210-6560-994
FAX +30-210-6545-525

MEXICO (Also serving Latin America)
McGraw-Hill Interamericana Editores
S.A. de C.V.
TEL +525-1500-5108
FAX +525-117-1589
http://www.mcgraw-hill.com.mx
carlos_ruiz@mcgraw-hill.com

SINGAPORE (Serving Asia)
McGraw-Hill Book Company
TEL +65-6863-1580
FAX +65-6862-3354
http://www.mcgraw-hill.com.sg
mghasia@mcgraw-hill.com

SOUTH AFRICA
McGraw-Hill South Africa
TEL +27-11-622-7512
FAX +27-11-622-9045
robyn_swanepoel@mcgraw-hill.com

SPAIN
McGraw-Hill/
Interamericana de España, S.A.U.
TEL +34-91-180-3000
FAX +34-91-372-8513
http://www.mcgraw-hill.es
professional@mcgraw-hill.es

UNITED KINGDOM, NORTHERN, EASTERN, & CENTRAL EUROPE
McGraw-Hill Education Europe
TEL +44-1-628-502500
FAX +44-1-628-770224
http://www.mcgraw-hill.co.uk
emea_queries@mcgraw-hill.com

ALL OTHER INQUIRIES Contact:
McGraw-Hill/Osborne
TEL +1-510-420-7700
FAX +1-510-420-7703
http://www.osborne.com
omg_international@mcgraw-hill.com

Sound Off!

Visit us at **www.osborne.com/bookregistration** and let us know what you thought of this book. While you're online you'll have the opportunity to register for newsletters and special offers from McGraw-Hill/Osborne.

We want to hear from you!

Sneak Peek

Visit us today at **www.betabooks.com** and see what's coming from McGraw-Hill/Osborne tomorrow!

Based on the successful software paradigm, Bet@Books™ allows computing professionals to view partial and sometimes complete text versions of selected titles online. Bet@Books™ viewing is free, invites comments and feedback, and allows you to "test drive" books in progress on the subjects that interest you the most.